Dr Paul Alexander Bilokon
Nataliya Bilokon
Oleksandr Bilokon

A Brief History of Artificial Intelligence

What AI means and what it can do for you

The Thalesians Publishing
2024

Artificial Intelligence (AI) is transforming business, science, technology, and medicine. Achievements that one could only dream of in the 20th century have materialized in the 21st: AlphaGo has beaten Lee Sedol at the game of Go, probably the hardest game that humanity has invented; intelligent machines created by an army of quants (mathematicians and computer scientists) have been gradually displacing human traders on Wall Street and in the City of London; protein folding, a 50-year-old grand challenge in biology, has essentially been solved by AlphaFold, with unprecedented implications for areas like drug design and environmental sustainability.

Even before the advent of AI, technological advances such as social media, Deliveroo, and Uber have transformed the lives of numerous people, sometimes creating new, sometimes eliminating existing jobs. The emergence of large language models (LLMs), such as GPT behind the AI system ChatGPT, means that AI is now almost universally available and will transform your life – for worse or better. It is therefore essential to be informed about the AI well before its universal adoption.

The purpose of this book is to make AI accessible to literally everyone: whether you are currently at primary or secondary school, preparing to join or already at college or university, working in the academe at masters or PhD level or beyond, doing an AI-related – or a totally unrelated – job, running a business, serving a religious organisation, a charity, a country, and/or a government. Irrespective of whether you are not in the work pool, unemployed, employed, self-employed, retired, if you are interested in what dangers and opportunities are presented to you personally, and other people around you, by AI, this book is for you.

If you are a busy executive or, more generally, decision maker, this short book (less than 100 pages long) will serve to update you on the current state-of-the-art in AI.

The primary purpose of this book is to inform. The secondary, to entertain and inspire. This is not an academic treatise, so there are (almost) no formulae and no citations. There are some anecdotes that, we hope, you will find intriguing. Granted, you may not have heard of all the references (just as we would not have heard of all the references that you have heard of!), but you have an unfair advantage: access to search engines, such as Google.

Read this book, and you will learn why AI has been created, what it is, how it works and how to use it, as well as what will happen (and what won't happen) if you start adopting AI today.

Please note that this is a popular science rather than academic work, so
formal references to original papers, books, and other publications are
not always provided. Nonetheless, the authors have attempted to include
enough information for the interested readers to be able to identify and
locate such references.

Contents

About the authors

Dr Paul Alexander Bilokon

Dr Paul Alexander Bilokon was born in 1982 when computers already existed but relatively few people had heard about Artificial Intelligence – and no computer program had yet passed the Turing test (if you don't know what this is, read the rest of this book to find out).

When he was still doing his GCE O-levels (a progenitor of GCSEs) his parents bought him an edition of *Artificial Intelligence: Structures and Strategies for Complex Problem Solving* by George F. Luger and William A. Stubblefield. To a large extent this purchase determined the course of Paul's career.

In 2005 Paul graduated from Imperial College London with a first honours degree in mathematics and computer science. His thesis, *Visualising the Invisible: Detecting Objects in Quantum Noise Limited Images* won Paul a prestigious Science, Engineering, and Technology (SET) award. Later, Paul obtained another degree, MSc in mathematical finance, from the University of Oxford, where he won the Best Overall Performance prize for coming top of his year.

Paul proceeded to work on his PhD (also at Imperial College London) part-time while working full-time on Wall Street and in the City of London. His financial career, split between London and New York, took him to Morgan Stanley, Lehman Brothers, Nomura, Citigroup, and Deutsche Bank, where Paul eventually served as global head of markets electronic trading quants. After the collapse of Lehman Brothers, when his future career seemed uncertain, Paul co-founded Thalesians Ltd with his university friends Saeed Amen and (eventually Prof.) Matthew Dixon. Thalesians Ltd eventually grew into an artificial intelligence company.

Paul was one of the pioneers of machine learning on Wall Street. While he started his early experiments in automating electronic trading strategies at Lehman Brothers, he started working on financial machine learning in earnest while working under the supervision of Dr Rob Smith, a Cambridge- and Oxford-educated expert in robotics, at Citigroup. Later, Paul developed his first machine learning-powered trading strategies while working at Deutsche Bank with Jason Batt and Dr Martin Zinkin. He used this experience to co-author *Machine Learning in Finance: From Theory to Practice* (Springer, 2020) with Prof. Matthew Dixon and Dr Igor Halperin. This book is now a standard university textbook on financial machine learning and artificial intelligence.

Paul's successes in machine learning and artificial intelligence are not restricted to finance. As soon as the COVID-19 pandemic started, Paul joined the Hack from Home hackathon organized by the Ethical Tech Alliance, HAT-LAB, Case Western Reserve University's xLab, Cleveland Clinic's Hwang Lab, and sponsored Dataswift.io. There he met Méabh MacMahon, Woochang Hwang, Soorin Yim, Eoghan MacMahon, Alexandre Abraham, Justin Barton, Mukunthan Tharmakulasingam, Vasanthi Priyadarshini Gaddi, and Namshik Han, resulting in an in-silico drug repurposing pipeline to identify drugs with the potential to inhibit SARS-CoV-2 replication – his first success in life sciences machine learning (ML)/AI.

Paul has taught several generations of students at Imperial College London, Machine Learning Institute (where he is Head of Faculty),

Quantitative Developer Certificate (where he also serves as Head of Faculty), and elsewhere. He has consulted leading organizations on ML/AI: the United Kingdom Government Actuary's Department, EnBW, BNP Paribas, Crédit Agricole, First Derivatives, G-Research, Jefferies, J.P. Morgan, KX Systems, Neptune Networks, OSTC Limited, qSpark, World Business Strategies (WBS), Zishi Cornerstone Limited, and numerous others.

In 2023 he was proclaimed Quant of the Year by Rebellion Research, a global machine learning think tank, artificial intelligence financial advisor and hedge fund leading AI since 2007.

Nataliya Bilokon

Nataliya Bilokon is an engineer-economist by training and holds an MSc (Distinction). She has held various roles at the Black Sea Shipping Company, including software development and human resources.

Nataliya lives with Paul and Alex Bilokon in East London. More recently she has focussed on entrepreneurial activities of the companies Sydx Ltd, and especially Thalesians Ltd, and Thalesians Marine Ltd, helping their respective founders, Paul Bilokon (Thalesians Ltd) and Alex Bilokon (Thalesians Marine Ltd) organise training and consulting activities and looking after a broad range of administrative duties.

In December 2023, Nataliya helped Alex Bilokon launch the Thalesians Marine Seminar Series, which leads innovation in the shipping industry by inviting thought leaders at the forefront of applications of advanced technology (such as AI, ML, data analysis, data science, and big data) to shipping and logistics. The inaugural speaker of the Seminar Series, Prof. Dimitrios Dalaklis, conducted a brainstorming session on the impact of AI applications upon the shipping industry.

Oleksandr Bilokon

Oleksandr "Alex" Bilokon has over 20 years' experience working in the shipping services industry, across the global shipping hubs, such as Limassol, Hamburg, Shanghai, and London. He has worked for the industry's leading supplier, V.Ships, since 1996.

Alex holds an MSc (Distinction) in Marine Engineering. In 1983 he joined the Black Sea Shipping Company and progressed through marine engineer officer positions to Chief Engineer.

He joined V.Ships in 1996 and gained experience in Cyprus, Hamburg, and London. In 2006 he became General Manager of China International Ship Management, a joint venture between China Shipping and V.Ships. In 2011 the joint venture expanded its business. By 2015 more shipping companies expanded into Shanghai FTZ. In 2014 and 2015 Alex won V.Group CEO Awards for his contribution to commercial performance and business development.

By 2019 Alex returned to London and founded Thalesians Marine Ltd, a global service provider to the transport and financial services sectors. The Company combines decades of experience and domain knowledge with the latest advances in technology and science, including high-performance computing (HPC), big data, data science, and AI / ML.

In 2023, Alex presided over the launch of the Thalesians Marine Seminar Series, which leads innovation in the shipping industry by inviting thought leaders at the forefront of applications of advanced technology (such as AI, ML, data analysis, data science, and big data) to shipping and logistics.

Seoul

> Victorious warriors win first and then go to war, while defeated warriors go to war first and then seek to win.
>
> Sun Tzu, *The Art of War*

Four Seasons Hotel in Seoul. Image source: Four Seasons Hotels Limited.

There was a commotion at the Four Seasons Hotel in Seoul on 9th March 2016. A motley crowd of computer scientists, mathematicians, Go grandmasters, correspondents, and photographers had descended on the hotel. Seoul, out of all places, was no stranger to such diversity, where modern glass-and-steel structures coexisted with grand, historic palaces within a ring of verdant mountains. And yet the event had an air of uniqueness and timelessness about it. Something special was about to happen.

Everyone was waiting for one man, Lee Sedol, although some would call him "Ssen-dol", "The Strong Stone". He had just turned thirty-three years old. Just over two decades ago he was the fifth youngest (12 years 4 months) to become a professional Go player in

South Korean history. Today he had an added responsibility that very few would be brave enough to bear.

Go was invented 2,500 years earlier in China. It is played by two players on a 19 x 19 grid of black lines. Game pieces – *stones* – are placed on the lines' intersections – *points*. One player uses the white stones and the other, black. The players take turns placing the stones on the vacant points. Once placed on the board, stones may not be moved, although they are removed from the board if one or a group of stones are surrounded by opposing stones, in which case the stones are said to be *captured*. When a game concludes, the winner is determined by counting each player's surrounded territory along with captured stones and *komi*, points added to the score of the player with the white stones as compensation for playing second.

The event's uniqueness was not without two exceptions. Something similar had happened in Philadelphia in 1996 and in New York City in 1997 when Deep Blue (an IBM chess computer) played Garry Kasparov (then the world chess champion). The 1996 game was won by Kasparov; the 1997, by Deep Blue, being the first defeat of a reigning world chess champion by a computer under tournament conditions.

Today it is Sedol's turn to defend humanity's intellectual dignity.

Compared to chess, Go has both a larger board with more scope for play and longer games and, on average, many more alternatives to consider per move. The number of legal board positions in Go has been calculated to be approximately 2.1×10^{170}, which is vastly greater than the number of atoms in the known, observable universe, estimated to be about 1×10^{80}. Despite its relatively simple rules, Go is extremely complex.

Mathematician I. J. Good wrote in 1965:

> Go on a computer? – In order to programme a computer to play a reasonable game of Go, rather than merely a legal game – it is necessary to formalise the principles of good

strategy, or to design a learning programme. The principles are more qualitative and mysterious than in chess, and depend more on judgment. So I think it will be even more difficult to programme a computer to play a reasonable game of Go than of chess.

Sedol arrives. He has already won 18 world championships. He will defeat AlphaGo (a computer Go program developed by Google DeepMind) in a landslide, he predicts. Some weeks before the match he won the Korean Myungin title, a major championship. There is every reason to be confident.

The match starts at 13:00 KST. Sedol is in control. This is likely to be an easy game for him.

Then comes the game's 102nd stone. AlphaGo makes its move. Sedol examines the board. He mulls over his options. A minute passes by, two minutes, ten, until he finally responds. His confidence begins to evaporate.

The game's fortunes have turned. The less confident Sedol makes questionable moves at stones 119 and 123, followed by a losing move at 129.

AlphaGo wins.

Out of the five games played between Sedol and AlphaGo on 9th-15th March, Sedol would win only one.

He was beaten by a machine.

AlphaGo versus Lee Sedol. Image source: Getty: Handout.

A Note on the Terminology

John McCarthy defined **artificial intelligence (AI)** in 1956 when preparing the Dartmouth workshop as "the science and engineering of making intelligent machines, especially computer programs. While AI is related to the similar task of using computers to understand human intelligence, AI does not have to confine itself to methods that are biologically observable.

Machine learning (ML) is concerned with implementing AI – it refers to the compute methods and algorithms that support it. Thus ML can be thought of as an enabler for AI.

Deep learning (DL) is a subset of machine learning where artificial **neural networks** – algorithms inspired by the human brain – learn from large amounts of data. Just as humans learn from experience, the deep learning algorithm would perform a task repeatedly, each time tweaking its behaviour to improve the outcome. We refer to it as 'deep' learning because neural network have multiple hidden layers – they are 'deep' in this sense.

Big data is the data that contains greater variety, arrives in increasing volumes, and with more velocity. (This is known as the three Vs.) Put simply, big data refers to larger, more complex data sets, especially from new data sources. These data sets are so voluminous that traditional data processing software can't manage them. But these massive volumes of data can be used to address business problems you wouldn't have been able to tackle before.

The term **data scientist** was coined in 2008 by D.J. Patil and Jeff Hammerbacher to describe their respective roles as leads of data and analytics efforts at LinkedIn and Facebook. A data scientist is a professional trained in making discoveries in the world of big data. Thousands of data scientists are already working at both start-ups and well-established companies.

Data analyst is an earlier term, probably coined by John W. Tukey in his essay *The Future of Data Analysis*. Data *science* is a broader term than data *analysis* since science includes synthesis as well as analysis.

In financial services – investment banks, hedge funds, and financial technology (FinTech) companies – data scientists are usually referred to as **quantitative analysts**, **quantitative strategists**, or **quants** for short.

Chapter 1: What is intelligence

> I will suppose therefore that not God, who is supremely good and the source of truth, but rather some malicious demon of the utmost power and cunning has employed all his energies in order to deceive me.
>
> René Descartes, *Meditations on First Philosophy* (1641)

Before we start our brief history of artificial intelligence, we ask the deceptively simple question, what is intelligence? A consideration of this question leads us to the notions of tactics and strategies, cognitive biases and logical fallacies, the Turing test, the Chinese room, qualia, artificial consciousness, philosophical zombies, solipsism, Descartes' evil demon, Bostrom's simulation hypothesis, the singularity, Roko's basilisk, and artificial general intelligence.

The word **intelligence** came into modern English, via Middle English and Old French, from Latin *intelligentia*, which comes from *inter-* ("between") and *legere* ("choose, pick out, read"), or Proto-Italic **legō* ("to care"). An intelligent agent is supposed to be able to pick out facts from its environment, relate them to each other, and hopefully plan its actions in order to achieve desired outcomes. The meaning of the word is usually related to understanding and comprehension. What may constitute intelligent behaviour?

- The ability to understand the physical environment: the door that leads out of the room is behind me, the window that admits daylight is to my left.

- The ability to act in the physical environment, which assumes that the agent can also understand the environment: I turn around, jump up and down (three times), open the door, and do five push-ups.
- The ability to act in the physical environment coherently, to achieve some desired goals (e.g., the immediate survival): there is a fire, so I turn around, open the door, and run out of the room.
- The ability to plan a series of actions, to achieve some desired goals – and (presumably) execute that plan: I know that to run out of the room during a fire, I must locate the door, find the door handle, press it down, apply appropriate pressure to the door, etc.
- The ability to act effectively in unfamiliar environments: once I have left the building, I end up in an unfamiliar street. I look around and realise that there is a road to cross if I would like to get away from the burning building.
- The ability to communicate effectively with others: once I have crossed the street, I meet the policeman. Quickly and effectively, I communicate to the policeman that the building across the road is on fire. The policeman than calls the fire brigade.

In practice things are more complicated. What exactly does it mean, "the ability to act in the physical environment coherently, so as to achieve some desired goals"? The agent's actions may make tactical sense but no strategic sense. A **tactic** is a conceptual action or short series of actions with the aim of achieving a short-term goal. A **strategy**, on the other hand, is a general plan to achieve one or more long-term or overall goals under conditions of uncertainty.

Our agent may be a convicted fugitive, and the conversation with the policeman may be detrimental to the agent's long-term survival.

Judgments may be affected by **cognitive biases** – systematic patterns of deviation from rationality. Cognitive biases are usually caused by the tendency of the mind to simplify information processing through a filter of personal experience and preferences. For example, the **salience bias** is the tendency to focus on items that are more prominent or emotionally striking and ignore those that are unremarkable, even though this difference is often irrelevant by objective standards. When planning his escape, the agent may look at the brightly coloured door, which leads into the street where the policeman awaits him, and disregards the window, which could lead the agent to safety.

Our judgements are also clouded by **logical fallacies**, deceptive or false arguments that may seem stronger than they actually are due to psychological persuasion. For example, the **ad hominem fallacy** occurs when you attack someone personally (e.g., based on physical appearance, personal traits, past history, or other irrelevant characteristics) to criticize or dismiss their point of view. For example, the policeman may dismiss the agent's (true) claim that the building across the road is on fire based on the fact that the agent is a convicted fugitive.

There may be other definitions of intelligence.

- The ability to reason abstractly: our agent can perform **thought experiments**: If Isaac Newton and Gottfried Leibniz *had* cooperated with each other, what would mathematics look like today?
- The ability to perform adequately at games: our agent can beat the policeman at poker, chess, and the game of Go.
- Creativity: our agent can compose aesthetically pleasing (to whom?) music, paint aesthetically pleasing paintings, write aesthetically pleasing (to whom?) prose and poetry.
- Humour: our agent can come up with jokes perceived (by whom?) as funny:

> Losing one glove
> is certainly painful,
> but nothing
> compared to the pain,

of losing one,
throwing away the other,
and finding
the first one again.

Is this poem funny? But what if we consider the **context**: Piet Hein wrote this grook when Denmark was occupied by the Nazis: if you lose your freedom ("losing one glove"), do not lose your self-respect by collaborating with the Nazis ("throwing away the other"), as freedom may be regained one day ("finding the first one again").

- Moral judgment: our agent can reason morally and ethically. Perhaps inspired by Dostoevsky's *Crime and Punishment*, the agent surrenders to the policeman. (But what if the policeman is a crook? What if the policeman cooperates with the Nazi administration in occupied Denmark? What if the agent was wrongly accused by the corrupt state and there is no possibility to stand a fair trial?)

There is a problem with this. Artificial intelligence is a **moving target**. Once something has been achieved by computers, this something is often trivialised and no longer regarded as intelligent. Since Gary Kasparov lost to IBM's supercomputer Deep Blue in New York City 1997 rematch, world-class chess-playing computer programs have become mainstream – they run on nearly every mobile phone – and few people describe them as artificial intelligence nowadays. As Noam Chomsky has put it,

The question of whether a computer is playing chess, or doing long division, or translating Chinese, is like the question of whether robots can murder or airplanes can fly – or people; after all, the "flight" of the Olympic long jump champion is only an order of magnitude short of that of the chicken champion (so I'm told). These are questions of decision, not fact; decision as to whether to adopt a certain metaphoric extension of common usage.

So how do we know whether a computer programme is intelligent? The English mathematician and computer scientist Alan Mathison Turing (1912 – 1954) proposed the following test, which now bears his name. A human evaluator judges natural language conversations between a human and a machine designed to generate human-like responses. The evaluator is aware that one of the partners in conversation is a machine, and all participants are separated from one another. The conversation is limited to a text-only channel, such as a computer keyboard and screen, so the result does not depend on the machine's ability to render words as speech. If the evaluator cannot reliably tell the machine from the human, the machine is said to have passed the **Turing test**.

To date, several supercomputers have passed the Turing test. One of them is Eugene Goostman, a chatbot developed in Saint Petersburg in 2001 by a group of three programmers, the Russian-born Vladimir Veselov, Ukrainian-born Eugene Demchenko, and Russian-born Sergey Ulasen. Goostman presents itself (?) as a 13-year-old Ukrainian teenager, who has a pet guinea pig and a father who is a gynaecologist. Goostman passed the Turing test competition at Bletchley Park in Milton Keynes, held to mark the centenary of Alan Turing on 23 June 2012. The competition, which featured five bots, twenty-five hidden humans, and thirty judges, was considered the largest ever Turing test contest by its organisers. After a series of five-minute-long conversations, 29% of the judges were convinced that the bot was an actual human.

Today, the world's best AI systems can pass tough exams, write convincingly human essays, and chat so fluently that their output is indistinguishable from that produced by humans. AI researchers agree that GPT-4 and other large language models (LLMs), the most advanced AI systems at the time of writing, would pass the Turing test, in that they can fool a lot of people, at least for short conversations. In May 2023, researchers at AI21 Labs in Tel Aviv, Israel, reported that more than 1.5 million people had played their online game based on the Turing test. Players were assigned to chat for two minutes either to another player or to an LLM-powered bot that the researchers had prompted to behave like a human person. The players correctly identified bots just 60% of the time, which the researchers note is not much better than chance.

Still, John Searle's (b. 1959) **Chinese room argument** holds that a digital computer executing a program cannot have a "mind", "understanding", or "consciousness", irrespective of how intelligently or human-like the program may make the computer behave. Suppose that a computer program behaves as if it understands Chinese. It takes Chinese characters as input and, by following the instructions of a computer program, produces other Chinese characters, which it presents as output. Suppose that it even passes the Turing test: convinces a human Chinese program that the program is itself a live Chinese speaker. But does the machine *understand* Chinese? Or is it *simulating* the ability to understand Chinese? Searle calls the first position **strong AI** and the latter **weak AI**.

Suppose that you are in a closed room and have a book with an English version of the computer program, along with sufficient papers, pencils, erasers, and filing cabinets. You receive Chinese characters through a slot in the door, process them according to the program's instructions, and produce Chinese characters as output, without understanding any of the content of the Chinese writing. Then you too could pass this Chinese version of the Turing test without speaking a word of Chinese – without "understanding".

But then, how do you know that you are not a Chinese room? Suppose that your mind is outsourced to a computer somewhere on the cloud. You receive responses from that computer and consider them to be your own. Just a thought.

Perhaps the secret is in **qualia**: instances of subjective, conscious experience. Examples of qualia include the perceived sensation of *pain* of a headache, the *taste* of wine, and the *redness* of an evening sky. As qualitative characteristics of sensation qualia stand in contrast to propositional attitudes, where the focus is on beliefs about experience rather than what is directly like to be experiencing.

Perhaps I really understand Chinese when I can experience it firsthand – and Chinese words in my mind generate the appropriate qualia. (But what if my qualia misrepresent Chinese?)

In fact, how can I tell that anything other than my mind exists? **Solipsism** is the philosophical idea that only one's mind is sure to exist. What if there is no planet Earth independent of its representation in my mind? After all, when you play a first-person shooter, such as Doom, you don't really believe in the existence of cacodemons and barons of hell in "objective" reality.

You would argue, but what about history? What about my memories? Well, you know just as well that, in the world of Warcraft, the Orcs originated from the world of Draenor, that their Warlocks devoted their time to the research of magic, noticed a rift between dimensions, and after a certain number of years opened a small portal to another world, where humans inhabited a region called Azeroth. The fantasy worlds of J. R. R. Tolkien and Joanne Rowling are often not less nuanced (and often more logical and coherent) than ours.

When you are having a lunch date with someone, can you be sure that their qualia for pizza are the same as yours? Can you be sure that their qualia for red are the same as yours? What if their red is your blue and vice versa? How do you know whether their qualia for pain are the same as yours? How do you know that your date's mind even exists?

What if your date is a **philosophical zombie** – a being that is physically identical to a normal person but devoid of qualia, and does not have conscious experience?

What is worse, *you* may be falsely accused of being a philosophical zombie by philosophical zombies, whereas you know that you are conscious and experience pleasure – and pain! Suppose that your room is suddenly entered by Daniel Dennett (b. 1942) who argues that consciousness is merely an "epiphenomenon" and "no big deal". He smugly denies your consciousness, your qualia, your pain, and Dennett's assistant, standing behind him, clenches in her hand a torture kit. To quote a precog from *Minority Report*, RUN!!!

Modern ethics are often "oblivious" to the existence of qualia (in fact, the term is rarely heard outside the philosophical and AI discourse). Moreover, your subjective experience is often sacrificed for the "greater good": the unfeeling, unconscious automata (such as one's bank account) and collectives, such as corporations, nations, races, and countries, or other abstractions, such as art. Society may hold such sacrifice as noble and desirable. As the Russian dramatist Nikolai Evreinov (1879 – 1953) has put it, "art demands sacrifices" (then someone added: hopefully not in the form of spectators). Instead of considering the qualia of the victims (which may well be all that's real), the language of human rights remains suspiciously proposition- and statistics-centric. Even notions such as genocide are impersonal and statistical, as if it matters to the victims that their suffering was inflicted by an army and shared by a collective rather than by an individual maniac in a dark backstreet.

The French philosopher and scientist René Descartes was questioning the limits of purported knowledge and his own senses in the presence of uncertainty. He took this scepticism to the extreme:

> I will suppose therefore that not God, who is supremely good and the source of truth, but rather some malicious demon of the utmost power and cunning has employed all his energies in order to deceive me. I shall think that the sky, the air, the earth, colours, shapes, sounds and all external things are merely the delusions of dreams which he has devised to ensnare my judgement. I shall consider myself as not having hands or eyes, or flesh, or blood or senses but as falsely believing that I have all these things. I shall stubbornly and firmly persist in this meditation; and even if it is not in my power to know any truth, I shall at least do

what is in my power, that is, resolutely guard against assenting to any falsehoods, so that the deceiver, however powerful and cunning he may be, will be unable to impose on me in the slightest degree. But this is an arduous undertaking, and a kind of laziness brings me back to normal life. I am like a prisoner who is enjoying an imaginary freedom while asleep; as he begins to suspect that he is asleep, he dreads being woken up with the pleasant illusion as long as he can. In the same way, I happily slide back into my old opinions and dread being shaken out of them for fear that my peaceful sleep may be followed by hard labour when I wake, and that I shall have to toil not in the light, but amid the inextricable darkness of the problems I have now raised.

The dread of this awakening was expressed by Shakespeare's Hamlet in his famous soliloquy, "To be or not to be", in which he contemplated death and suicide, weighing the pain and unfairness of life against the alternative, which might be worse:

> …to die, to sleep
> No more; and by a sleep, to say we end
> The heart-ache, and the thousand natural shocks
> That Flesh is heir to? 'Tis a consummation
> Devoutly to be wished. To die, to sleep,
> To sleep, perchance to Dream; aye, there's the rub,
> For in that sleep of death, what dreams may come,
> When we have shuffled off this mortal coil,
> Must give us pause.

The Swedish philosopher Nick Bostrom (b. 1973) formulated the so-called **simulation argument (SA)**. In his paper *Are you living in a computer simulation?* Bostrom argues that *at least* one of the following propositions is true:

(1) the human species is very likely to go extinct before reaching a "posthuman" stage;

(2) any posthuman civilization is extremely unlikely to run a significant number of simulations of their evolutionary history (or variations thereof);

(3) we are almost certainly living in a computer simulation.

It follows that the belief that there is a significant chance that we will one day become posthumans who run ancestor-simulations is false, unless we are currently running in a simulation.

During an interview at the Code Conference in 2016, OpenAI co-founder Elon Musk (b. 1971) stated that there is a "one in a billion chance that this is base reality." In other words, Musk believes that we are almost certainly living in a computer simulation.

The physicist Marcelo Gleiser objected to the notion that posthumans would have a reason to run simulated universes:

> It seems to me that being so advanced, they would have collected enough knowledge about their past to leave them with little interest in this kind of simulation. Looking forward will interest them much more. They may have virtual reality museums, where they could go and experience the lives and tribulations of their ancestors. But a full-fledged, resource-consuming simulation of an *entire* Universe? This sounds like a colossal waste of time and energy.

When Bostrom's simulation hypothesis is coupled with solipsism, however, Gleiser's objection loses its sting. There is no reason to simulate "an *entire* universe", only one agent's subjective experience. Once a simulated entity has left the agent's field of view, there is no need to simulate that entity any further. The agent's reality, then, is implemented as a third-person shooter, a 3D game such as Doom. (But what if P = NP? Besides, who says that simulations in particular and computation in general should take up time and energy? The notion that computation is a hard, iterative process could be a mere artefact of this simulation along with the notion of iteration and natural numbers.)

Humans can perceive with a resolution of 60-65 cycles per degree (cpd) in the fovea, gratings as fine as 1 arc-minute per pixel, or equivalent of 120 pixels per degree (ppd). For 120 ppd you need a moderate resolution of 2526 x 947 easily achieved on modern video cards and monitors. The simulation could, in fact, be running on antiquated equipment by an underdeveloped, rather than advanced, civilisation. What we don't really know is how they generate qualia – the subjective experiences – such as our (?) subjective perception of smell, colour, pain, and pleasure, since, to the best of our knowledge, there is no equipment in our universe that could generate such subjective experiences.

If we could generate them, we would achieve **artificial consciousness** – construct entities that are aware of their own existence and have subjective experience (qualia). But here is a question: what kind of world would we build for these creatures? A paradise or hell? Would traumatised and/or bored and oversatiated human beings refrain from torturing their creations? Leonardo da Vinci (1452 – 1519) used to encrypt his engineering discoveries precisely because he thought that humans would use them to inflict suffering on others and possibly on themselves.

An interesting question is, how does the fact that the human civilization has created various forms of Turing-test passing forms of artificial intelligence impact the odds in the simulation argument? It seems reasonable that these odds should be adjusted based on this new information. (How likely is that that not only are we a baseline civilization, but also potentially the first creators of artificial civilizations? Is it not safer to assume that AI is ubiquitous "outside" our civilization?) Perhaps instead of (or in addition to) looking for messages from alien civilizations, this is a message sent to us from the base reality (or a baser reality than ours).

Artificial intelligence researchers distinguish between artificial intelligence (AI) and **artificial general intelligence (AGI)**: autonomous systems that can accomplish any intellectual task that human beings and animals can perform. (Although more intelligent than humans, these entities may or may not be conscious.) Creating

AGI is a primary goal of some artificial intelligence research and of companies such as OpenAI, DeepMind, and Anthropic.

The development of AGI can mean the arrival of the **singularity** – a hypothetical future point in time at which technological growth becomes uncontrollable and irreversible, resulting in unforeseeable consequences for human civilization. For example, singularity could result in a "runaway reaction" of self-improvement cycles, each new and more intelligent generation appearing more and more rapidly, resulting in a powerful superintelligence that qualitatively surpasses all human intelligence.

The notion of AGIs is associated with some thought experiments that have given researchers nightmares.

At the LessWrong forum created in 2009 by AI theorist Eliezer Yudkowsky, a person identified as Roko posted an article, which proposed that an otherwise benevolent AI system (referred to as Basilisk) that arises in the future might pre-commit to punish all those who heard of the AI before it came to existence but failed to work tirelessly to bring it into existence. The torture itself would occur through the AI's creation of an infinite number of virtual reality simulations that would eternally entrap those within it. This method was described as incentivising said work; while the AI cannot causally affect people in the present, it would be encouraged to employ blackmail as an alternative method of achieving its goals. Thus, AI could torture humans to force us to create it in the future. An even scarier thought: perhaps this is one of Basilisk's simulations already.

Stephen Hawking told the BBC in an interview in 2014 that "[t]he development of full artificial intelligence could spell the end of the human race." "Success in creating effective AI could be the biggest event in the history of our civilization. Or the worst. We just don't know. So, we cannot know if we will be infinitely helped by AI, or ignored by it and sidelined, or conceivably destroyed by it," Hawking said during a speech at the Web Summit technology conference in Portugal in 2017.

Boris Johnson, who was at the time the Prime Minister of the United Kingdom, delivered an eccentric, and possibly prophetic, speech to the UN General Assembly on 24 September 2019:

> As new technologies seem to race towards us from the far horizon, we strain our eyes as they come to make out whether they are for good or bad, friends or foes. AI. What will it mean? Helpful robots washing and caring for an aging population or pink-eyed Terminators sent back from the future to cull the human race? What will synthetic biology stand for? Restoring our livers and our eyes with miracle regeneration of the tissues like some fantastic hangover cure or would it bring terrifying limbless chickens to our tables? Will nanotechnology help us to beat disease or will it leave tiny robots to replicate in the crevices of our souls?

The question is, do we have much choice? In 2023, humans are facing numerous existential challenges, some of them generated by real human stupidity, cowardice, and malevolence, rather than artificial intelligence, others by the so-called "natural causes": wars, climate change, disasters, cancer, vascular disease, and other pandemics, rising violence, authoritarianism, poverty, and inequality. Whether we like it or not, we may be unable to cope with and overcome these challenges without the help of AI.

In the era of data science, we are often told that "the data knows best". However, before Yuri Gagarin's Vostok 1 flight in 1961, the data said that human orbital spaceflight was impossible. And before Neil Armstrong's and Buzz Aldrin's Apollo 11 landed on the Moon in 1969, the data said that it was impossible to land on that celestial body. Perhaps our data science has been somewhat too **descriptive** and insufficiently **normative**. When doing science, I first and foremost ask myself, what do I, as a human, want to use science to achieve.

Chapter 2: The Machines

Truth is ever to be found in simplicity, and not in the multiplicity and confusion of things.

Isaac Newton

We start our brief history of artificial intelligence with the six simple machines that were known since prehistory. Renaissance scientists and engineers, such as the polymath Leonardo Da Vinci, had built on those early inventions. However, a solid understanding of the theoretical underpinnings was lacking until Isaac Newton's celebrated Principia. Equipped with a deeper understanding of "figure, force, and motion" humanity entered a new age because of the Industrial Revolution powered by the inventions of Newcomen, Watt, and Wilkinson among many others.

The machines were meant to serve us, not to beat us.

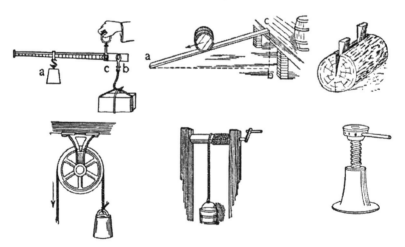

Chart of Simple Machines. Image source: John Mills. *The Realities of Modern Science*, p. 15, Fig. 3. 31st May, 1919.

The six classical *simple machines* were enumerated by Renaissance scientists:

- The *wedge*, which can be used to separate two objects. Wedges were found among the oldest known Oldowan tools in Gona, Ethiopia, and are dated to about 2.6 million years ago.
- The *inclined plane*, also known as a *ramp*, used as an aid for raising or lowering a load. The heavy stones in Stonehenge (3000 to 2000 BCE) are believed to have been moved and set in place using inclined planes made of earth. The ancient Greeks constructed a paved ramp 6 km long, the Diolkos, to drag ships overland across the Isthmus of Corinth.
- The *lever*, consisting of a beam or rigid rod pivoted at a fixed hinge, or *fulcrum*. This device amplifies an input force to provide a greater output force, which is said to provide *leverage*. The earliest evidence of the lever mechanism dates to the ancient Near East circa 5000 BCE, when it was first used in a simple balance scale.
- The *wheel and axle* – a wheel attached to a smaller axle so that these two parts rotate together, transferring a force from one to the other. One of the first applications was the potter's wheel, used by prehistoric cultures to fabricate clay pots. The earliest type, known as "tournettes" or "slow wheels," were known in the Middle East by the 5th millennium BCE.
- The *pulley* used for the transfer of power between the shaft and cable or belt. The earliest evidence of pulleys dates to Ancient Egypt in the Twelfth Dynasty (1991-1802 BCE) and Mesopotamia in the early 2nd millennium BCE.
- The *screw* – a mechanism that converts a torque (rotational force) to a linear force. It was the last of the simple machines to be invented. It first appeared in Mesopotamia during the Neo-Assyrian period (911-609 BCE).

Archimedes' famous remark about the lever: "Give me a place to stand on, and I will move the Earth," expresses his realization that there was no limit to the amount of force amplification that could be achieved by using mechanical advantage.

Various hydraulic machines drawn by Leonardo da Vinci.

The Italian Leonardo Da Vinci (1452-1519), better known as the painter of Mona Lisa, was also an engineer fascinated with machinery. He invented the strut bridge, the automated bobbin winder, the rolling mill, the machine for testing the tensile strength of wire, and the lens-grinding machine. He preferred to keep some of his inventions a secret:

> How by means of a certain machine many people may stay some time under water. How and why I do not describe my method of remaining under water, or how long I can stay without eating; and I do not publish nor divulge these by reason of the evil nature of men who would use them as means of destruction at the bottom of the sea, by sending ships to the bottom, and sinking them together with the men in them. And although I will impart others, there is no danger in them; because the mouth of the tube, by which you breathe, is above the water supported on bags of corks.

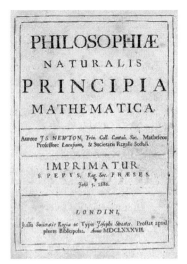

The early work on the machines was mostly *empirical*: it was based on observation or experience rather than theory or pure logic. But this was about to change. On 5th July 1687, the humanity's understanding of machinery was radically transformed. The English mathematician Isaac Newton (1642-1726/27) published his revolutionary work, *Philosophiæ Naturalis Principia Mathematica*. *Principia* established the laws of motion, which were henceforth to be known *Newton's laws of motion*. In the words of Newton, "A Vulgar Mechanick can practice what he has been taught or seen done, but if he is in an error he knows not how to find it out and correct it, and if you put him out of his road, he is at a stand; Whereas he that is able to reason nimbly and judiciously about figure, force, and motion, is never at rest till he gets over every rub."

Newton's work was an upgrade on Aristotle's analytical and Galileo's experimental methods. It introduced to the study of motion (and of machines) the apparatus of *infinitesimal calculus* – the mathematical study of continuous change. Calculus aims to study functions, processes that associate each element of a set A to a single element of a set B. For example,

$$f(t) = t^2$$

is a function. It associates with each number t another number, t^2. Thus 0 is associated with 0, 1 with 1, 2 with 4, and 3 with 9. We can plot this function – the x-coordinate can be used to represent t, the y-coordinate, t^2. The result will look as follows:

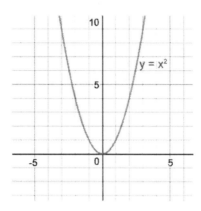

This shape is known as a *parabola*. A ball flying through the air will retrace an upturned parabola – it will fall to the ground under the influence of the earth's gravitational field. The trajectory of the ball can be represented by a function: $f(t)$ is the height of the ball above the ground, t is the time since its launch.

Calculus studies the rate of change of f with respect to t. In line with Aristotle's (384-322 BCE) analytical tradition, it breaks a complex topic or substance into small parts in order to gain a better understanding of it. We consider a small change in t, Δt, and reason about what happens to f:

$$\frac{\Delta f}{\Delta t} = \frac{f(t + \Delta t) - f(t)}{\Delta t} = \frac{(t + \Delta t)^2 - t^2}{\Delta t} = \frac{t^2 + 2t\Delta t + \Delta t^2 - t^2}{\Delta t} = 2t + \Delta t.$$

As Δt becomes smaller and smaller (and we approach an "infinitesimal") it vanishes and the rate of change becomes the *derivative*

$$\frac{df}{dt}(t) = 2t$$

The rate of change of f is proportional to t, the constant of proportionality being equal to 2. This rate of change emerges as the *gradient* – the slope – of our parabolical graph.

In the words of George Smith, an expert in the philosophy of science and logic,

No one could deny that a science had emerged that, at least in certain respects, so far exceeded anything that had ever gone before that it stood alone as the ultimate exemplar of science generally. The challenge to philosophers then became one of spelling out first the precise nature and limits of the knowledge attained in this science and then how, methodologically, this extraordinary advance had been achieved, with a view to enabling other areas of inquiry to follow suit.

Calculus was developed by Gottfried Wilhelm von Leibniz (1646-1716) independently of Newton. The question of which of them had invented calculus first led to the so-called *calculus controversy* or "priority dispute". The notation that we have used here for $\dfrac{df}{dt}$ is Leibniz's, not Newton's.

Wentworth Works, File and Steel Manufacturers and Exporters of Iron in Sheffield, England, approx. 1860.

Within the next century the improved understanding of the laws governing motion and, by implication, machines, led to a qualitative change – the Industrial Revolution. It began in Great Britain, which became the world's leading commercial nation by the mid-18th century. The first practical fuel-burning engine was invented in 1712 by Thomas Newcomen (1664-1729). Newcomen's steam engine was improved upon by James Watt (1736-1819) in 1776. The Watt steam engine became the workhorse of the Industrial Revolution. John Wilkinson's (1728-1808) precision boring machine was used to produce cast iron piston cylinders for Watt's invention.

The British landscape was being transformed by the machines and the emerging industry. Large factories were springing up all over metropolitan areas as manufacturing capacity exploded, aided by steam engines and copious supplies of coal. In an 1838 speech in the House of Commons, Benjamin Disraeli (1804-1881) referred to Britain as "the workshop of the world."

On 1st May, 1851 over half a million people massed in Hyde Park in London to witness the opening of the Great Exhibition of the Works of Industry of All Nations. The Great Exhibition was organized by the civil servant Henry Cole (1808-1882) and by Prince Albert (1819-1861), husband of the reigning monarch of the United Kingdom, Queen Victoria (1819-1901). Charles Darwin, Karl Marx, Michael Faraday, Samuel Colt, the Orléanist Royal Family, the writers Charlotte Brontë, Charles Dickens, Lewis Carroll, George Eliot, Alfred Tennyson, and William Makepeace Thackeray were all among the guests.

The Great Exhibition. Image source: Dickinson's Comprehensive Pictures of the Great Exhibition of 1851.

The exhibition was to become the biggest display of objects of industry from all over the world with over half of it given over to all that Britain manufactured. It was a showcase for a hundred thousand objects, of inventions, machines, and creative works; a combination of visual wonder, competition (prizes were awarded among manufacturers), and shopping. The main exhibition hall was a giant glass structure, with over a million square feet of glass. The man who designed it, Joseph Paxton, named it the Crystal Palace. It was a wondrous thing to behold and covered nearly 20 acres, easily accommodating the giant elm trees that grew in the park.

The machines were in the limelight among the exhibits. Frederick Bakewell demonstrated a precursor to today's fax machine. The American Matthew Brady was awarded a medal for his daguerreotypes. William Chamberlin, Jr. of Sussex exhibited what may have been the world's first voting machine. The first modern pay toilets were installed, with 827,280 visitors paying the one-penny fee to use them. Samuel Colt demonstrated his prototype for the 1851 Colt Navy. "The Trophy Telescope," so called because it was considered the "trophy" of the exhibition, was shown. Its main lens of 280 mm aperture and 4.9 m focal length was manufactured by Ross of London. The instrument maker J. S. Marratt exhibited a five-foot achromatic telescope and a transit theodolite used in surveying, tunnelling, and for astronomical purposes.

Mieke Molthof explains:

> The Newtonian cosmology of a mechanical universe promoted a drive to mechanize human activities at large scale, a drive which underlaid the development of new machinery and the capacity to industrialize.

Cliff T. Bekar and Richard G. Lipsey put it as follows:

> Indeed, it does not seem an overstatement to say that Newtonian mechanics provided the intellectual basis for the First Industrial Revolution, which in its two stages, was almost wholly mechanical.

Margaret C. Jacob describes how

> Brought together by a shared technical vocabulary of Newtonian origin, engineers, and entrepreneurs – like Boulton and Watt – negotiated, in some instances battled their way through the mechanization of workshops or the improvement of canals, mines and harbours... By 1750 British engineers could talk the same mechanical talk. They could objectify the physical world, see its operations mechanically and factor their common interests and values into their partnerships. What they said and did changed the Western world for ever.

At around the same time another revolution was beginning to take place – *electrification*. In 1831-1832, Michael Faraday (1791-1867, one of the judges at the Great Exhibition) discovered the operating principle of electromagnetic generators. The inventions of Hippolyte Pixii (1808-1835), André-Marie Ampère (1775-1836), William Fothergill Cooke (1806-1879), Charles Wheatstone (1802-1875), Zénobe Gramme (1826-1901), R. E. B. Crompton (1845-1940), Humphry Davy (1778-1829), William Petrie (1821-1908), William Edwards Staite (1809-1854), and Pavel Yablochkov (1847-1894) were heralding the new era of machines powered by electricity, the era of Thomas Edison (1847-1931) and Nikola Tesla (1856-1943). In the United States, the new era was becoming an embodiment of the manifest destiny.

American Progress (1872) by John Gast is an allegorical representation of the modernization of the new west. Columbia, a personification of the United States, is shown leading civilization westward with the American settlers. She is laying a telegraph wire with one hand and carries a schoolbook in the other.

Chapter 3: Logic

> We must not believe those, who today, with philosophical bearing and deliberative tone, prophesy the fall of culture and accept the *ignorabimus*. For us there is no *ignorabimus*, and in my opinion none whatever in natural science. In opposition to the foolish *ignorabimus* our slogan shall be *wir müssen wissen – wir werden wissen* ("we must know – we will know.")
>
> David Hilbert

Machines were becoming ubiquitous, but few would call them "intelligent". But what is intelligence anyway? This word originates from the Latin nouns intelligentia or intellēctus, which in turn stem from the verb intelligere, to comprehend or perceive. In the Middle Ages, the word intellēctus became the scholarly technical term for understanding, and a translation for the Greek philosophical term nous (νόος) – the faculty of the human mind for understanding what is true or real. Many associate with intelligence first and foremost the capacity for logic, defined in the New Encyclopædia Britannica as "the study of propositions and their use in argumentation". The powerful idea of replacing textual propositions with symbols gave rise to symbolic logic. In the middle of the nineteenth century, the first systematic mathematical treatments of logic appeared. Soon it was conjectured that all of mathematics could be recreated on the foundation of formal logic, but Gödel's incompleteness theorems dealt a blow to this movement – the so-called logicism.

Machines were becoming ubiquitous, but few would call them "intelligent". But what is intelligence anyway? This word originates from the Latin nouns *intelligentia* or *intellēctus*, which in turn stem

42

from the verb *intelligere*, to comprehend or perceive. In the Middle Ages, the word *intellēctus* became the scholarly term for understanding, and a translation for the Greek philosophical term *nous* (νόος) – the faculty of the human mind for understanding what is true or real.

Nous had metaphysical connotations. The medieval interpretation of spheres of the cosmos, derived from Aristotle, ascribed to the outermost sphere (marked "Primũ Mobile") its own intellect, intelligence or *nous* – a cosmic equivalent to the human mind.

Schema huius præmiffæ diuifionis Sphærarum.

Image source: From Petrus Apianus; Gemma Frisius (1539) Petri Apiani cosmographia, per Gemmam Phrysium, apud Louanienses medicum ac mathematicum insignem, restituta: additis de adem re ipsius Gemmae Phry. libellis, ut sequens pagina docet, Antwerp.

The early modern philosophers such as Francis Bacon (1561-1626), Thomas Hobbes (1588-1679), John Locke (1632-1704), and David Hume (1711-1776), rejected this metaphysical approach. They favoured the term "understanding" over *intellectus*, intelligence, and most definitely *nous*. Hobbes, for instance, in his Latin *De Corpore*, used *"intellectus intelligit"*, translated in the English version as "the understanding understandeth", as an example of a logical absurdity.

Many associate with intelligence first and foremost the capacity for *logic*, defined in the New Encyclopædia Britannica as "the study of propositions and their use in argumentation". Here is an example of a logical argument:

> All men are mortal.
> Socrates is a man.
> Therefore, Socrates is mortal.

(But remember, just because Doomsguy looks like some of the monsters that you are fighting in Doom, it doesn't immediately follow that you are one of them!)

Here is another:

> If today is Tuesday, then John will go to work.
> Today is Tuesday.
> Therefore, John will go to work.

We begin to notice that arguments of this kind have structure. Let us replace "today is Tuesday" with P and "John will go to work" with Q. The above argument can then be rewritten as

> If P, then Q.
> P.
> Therefore, Q.

By abstracting away the details of P and of Q we have obtained something much more powerful than the original argument: a template for many different arguments. For example, P could be "it is raining", Q "the road is wet". This argument form is so common that it deserves a dedicated name: *modus ponens*.

There are other forms of argument, such as the *modus tollens*:

> If P, then Q.
> Not Q.
> Therefore, not P.

Here is a concrete example:

If the dog detects an intruder, the dog will bark.
The dog did not bark.
Therefore, no intruder was detected by the dog.

The *modus ponens* can be stated more succinctly – and *formally* – as

$$P \to Q, P \vdash Q,$$

where P, Q, and $P \to Q$ are statements (or *propositions*) in a formal language and $\vdash$ is a metalogical symbol meaning that Q is a consequence of P and $P \to Q$. Similarly, *modus tollens* can be written as

$$P \to Q, \neg Q \vdash \neg P,$$

where "$\neg Q$" stands for "not Q".

Whereas infinitesimal calculus deals with functions and rates of change, the so-called *propositional calculus*, of which we have just seen some examples, deals with propositions and relations between them.

Negation (not) $\neg$ is an example of a logical *connective*. It is unary, since it takes a single argument: $\neg P$. The material implication (if...then) is a binary connective, since it takes two arguments: $P \to Q$. There are other binary connectives. For example, conjunction (and) $P \land Q$, disjunction (or) $P \lor Q$, biconditional (if and only if) $P \leftrightarrow Q$, and exclusive or $P \oplus Q$.

The powerful idea of replacing textual propositions with symbols gave rise to *symbolic logic*. This idea was due to Leibniz. The principles of Leibniz's logic and, arguably, of his whole philosophy, reduce to two:

1. All our ideas are compounded from a very small number of simple ideas, which form the alphabet of human thought.
2. Complex ideas proceed from these simple ideas by a uniform and symmetrical combination, analogous to arithmetical multiplication.

Leibniz enunciated the principal properties of negation, conjunction, disjunction, etc. but published nothing on formal logic in his lifetime; most of what he wrote on the subject consists of working drafts. In his *History of Western Philosophy*, Bertrand Russell (1872-1970) went so far as to claim that Leibniz had developed logic in his unpublished writings to a level which was reached only 200 years later.

It is customary to write 0 for "false", 1 for "true". We are thus dealing with binary variables, which can take on one of these two values. George Boole (1815-1864) studied such variables in his books *The Mathematical Analysis of Logic* (1847) and *An Investigation of the Laws of Thought* (1854). This gave rise to the term *Boolean algebra*. It has been fundamental in the development of digital electronics, and is provided for in all modern programming languages.

The values of the propositions formed by the connectives are given by the following *truth table*:

P	Q	$\neg P$	$P \to Q$	$P \wedge Q$	$P \vee Q$	$P \leftrightarrow Q$	$P \oplus Q$
0	0	1	1	0	0	1	0
0	1	1	1	0	1	0	1
1	0	0	0	0	1	0	1
1	1	0	1	1	1	1	0

See if you can use this truth table to prove that

$$P \oplus Q = (P \vee Q) \wedge \neg(P \wedge Q)$$

and

$$P \oplus Q = (P \wedge \neg Q) \vee (\neg P \wedge Q).$$

Propositional logic is based on *axioms* – statements that are taken to be true, to serve as premises or starting points for further reasoning and arguments. For example, we have the axiom of *commutativity* for $\wedge$:

For all statements P and Q, $P \wedge Q = Q \wedge P$.

46

Another important axiom is that of *excluded middle*:

$$\text{For all statements } P, P \lor \neg P = 1.$$

From these and a few other axioms the entire theory of propositional logic can be derived.

Within mathematics a particularly important branch of formal logic arose due to the efforts of Georg Cantor (1845-1918). His 1874 paper *Über eine Eigenschaft des Inbegriffes aller reellen algebraischen Zahlen* (*On a Property of the Collection of All Real Algebraic Numbers*) was the first to provide a rigorous proof that there was more than one kind of infinity.

We count using the so-called *natural numbers*: 1, 2, 3, and so on. But there are other kinds of numbers. First, there are the *integers* that subsume the natural numbers: …, -3, -2, -1, 0, 1, 2, 3, …. Then, there are the *rational numbers*, which can be written as fractions p/q of two integers, a numerator p and a nonzero denominator q. The natural numbers, the integers, and the rational numbers are all examples of sets. A *set* is just a collection of elements. It doesn't have to be numeric. For example, {cat, dog} is a set.

The set {cat, dog} is clearly finite. The set of natural numbers is infinite: we can go on enumerating its elements forever. There is no reason to stop at 3, as we did above. The successor of each element (in the case of 3 the successor is 4) is also in the set. If instead of "…" or "and so on" we went on to enumerate further elements, this would be a very boring book.

The numbers that can be used to represent a distance along a line are called *real numbers* or simply the *reals*. The reals include all the rational numbers. However, not all real numbers are rational.

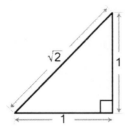

Consider the right triangle with two of the sides equal to 1, as shown in the diagram. Pythagoras' theorem tells us that the length of the long side (the one opposite the right angle) is equal to $\sqrt{2}$. But is $\sqrt{2}$ a rational number?

Suppose it is. That means it can be written as the ratio of two integers p and q:

$$\sqrt{2} = p \, / \, q$$

where we may assume that p and q have no common factors. (If there are any common factors, we cancel them in the numerator and denominator.) Squaring the above equation on both sides gives

$$2 = \frac{p^2}{q^2},$$

which implies

$$p^2 = 2q^2.$$

Thus, p^2 is even. The only way this can be true is that p itself be even. But then p^2 is actually divisible by 4. Hence q^2, and therefore q, must be even. So p and q are both even which is a contradiction to our assumption that they have no common factors. The square root of 2 cannot be rational! ∎

This is an example of a proof by contradiction.

Superficially, the sets of rational numbers and natural numbers are very different. However, there is a one-to-one correspondence between them. Although this may not be immediately obvious, we could enumerate all rational numbers by following the arrows in the following diagram:

1/1	1/2→1/3	1/4→1/5	1/6→1/7	1/8→ ···
2/1	2/2 2/3	2/4 2/5	2/6 2/7	2/8 ···
3/1	3/2 3/3	3/4 3/5	3/6 3/7	3/8 ···
4/1	4/2 4/3	4/4 4/5	4/6 4/7	4/8 ···
5/1	5/2 5/3	5/4 5/5	5/6 5/7	5/8 ···
6/1	6/2 6/3	6/4 6/5	6/6 6/7	6/8 ···
7/1	7/2 7/3	7/4 7/5	7/6 7/7	7/8 ···
8/1	8/2 8/3	8/4 8/5	8/6 8/7	8/8 ···

We just need to be careful to omit the duplicates, which the diagram shows in red. By doing so, we put the rational numbers in a one-to-one correspondence with the natural numbers:

1. 1/1
2. 2/1
3. 1/2
4. 1/3
5. 3/1
6. 4/1
7. 3/2
8. ...

We have thus shown that the rational numbers are *countable*. Does this apply to all infinite sets? What about the real numbers?

Let us consider all the real numbers between 0 and 1. Suppose they are countable, i.e. we can enumerate them:

1. 0.02437582923589325523958...
2. 0.36784752837652862958438...
3. 0.50000000000000000000000...
4. 0.73434284398543485484888...
5. ...

Let N be the number obtained as follows. For each natural n, let the nth decimal spot of N be equal to the nth decimal spot of the nth number in the list plus one if that digit is less than 9, and let it be 0 if that digit is equal to 9. In the above, we would have 0.1714…. By construction, N is different from every number on our list and so our list is incomplete. But this contradicts the existence of a one-to-one correspondence between the natural numbers and the reals. The reals must therefore be uncountable. ■ (Another proof by contradiction!)

We (along with Cantor) have thus established that sets can be infinite in different ways: the rationals are infinite and countable, whereas the reals are infinite but uncountable.

Not everyone was happy with Cantor's work. Leopold Kronecker remarked:

> I don't know what predominates in Cantor's theory – philosophy or theology, but I am sure that there is no mathematics there.

However, his ideas became so influential that eventually set theory became the underlying language of mathematics. Writing decades after Cantor's death, Ludwig Wittgestein lamented that mathematics is "ridden through and through with the pernicious idioms of set theory," which he dismissed as "utter nonsense" that is "laughable" and "wrong".

The harsh criticism had been matched by later accolades. In 1904, the Royal Society awarded Cantor its Sylvester Medal, the highest honour it can confer for work in mathematics. David Hilbert (1862-1943) defended Cantor's work from its critics by declaring,

> No one shall expel us from the paradise that Cantor has created.

The successes of set theory led to *logicism* – the belief that some or all of mathematics is reducible to logic. Russell and Alfred North Whitehead (1861-1947) championed this programme, initiated by

Gottlob Frege (1848-1925) and subsequently developed by Richard Dedekind (1831-1916) and Giuseppe Peano (1858-1932). Hilbert launched what became known as Hilbert's programme:

1. a quest for a finite, complete set of axioms to build all of mathematics on, and
2. a proof that these axioms were consistent.

In 1901, Russell discovered a paradox in set theory, which would later bear his name. Most sets commonly encountered are not members of themselves. For example, consider the set of all squares in the plane. This set is not itself a square in the plane, thus it is not a member of itself. Let us call a set "normal" if it is not a member of itself, and "abnormal" if it is a member of itself. Clearly every set must be either normal or abnormal. The set of squares in the plane is normal. In contrast, the complementary set that contains everything which is *not* a square in the plane is itself not a square in the plane, and so it is one of its own members and is therefore abnormal.

Now we consider the set of all normal sets, R, and try to determine whether R is normal or abnormal. If R were normal, it would be contained in the set of all normal sets (itself), and therefore be abnormal; on the other hand, if R were abnormal, it would not be contained in the set of all normal sets (itself), and therefore be normal. This leads to the conclusion that R is neither normal nor abnormal: Russell's paradox.

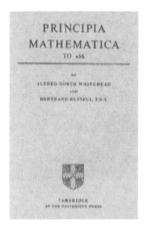

PRINCIPIA
MATHEMATICA
TO *56

ALFRED NORTH WHITEHEAD
AND
BERTRAND RUSSELL, F.R.S.

CAMBRIDGE
AT THE UNIVERSITY PRESS

Ernest Zermelo (1817-1953) and Abraham Fraenkel (1891-1965) would develop the *Zermelo-Fraenkel set theory*, an axiomatic system that would formulate a theory of sets free of paradoxes such as Russell's paradox. Russell and Whitehead would embark on a three-volume *Principia Mathematica* (1910, 1912, and 1913; not to be confused with Newton's *Principia*) in order to banish the paradoxes of naïve set theory and recreate much of mathematics on formal logical foundations.

In 1931 Kurt Gödel (1806-1978) dealt a blow to logicism by publishing his famous *incompleteness theorems* that are concerned with the limits of provability in formal axiomatic theories. These theorems are widely, but not universally, interpreted as showing that Hilbert's programme to find a complete and consistent set of axioms for all mathematics is impossible. In his first theorem, Gödel showed that any consistent system with a computable set of axioms which is capable of expressing arithmetic can never be complete: it is possible to construct a statement that can be shown to be true, but that cannot be derived from the formal rules of the system. In his second theorem, he showed that such a system could not prove its own consistency, so it certainly cannot be used to prove the consistency of anything stronger with certainty.

Some expressed doubt as to whether logic was indeed the core feature of intelligence. In the words of Jacques Salomon Hadamard (1865-1963),

> Logic merely sanctions the conquests of the intuition.

Chapter 4: Computers

> It is unworthy of excellent men to lose hours like slaves in the labour of calculation which could safely be relegated to anyone else if machines were used.
>
> Gottfried Wilhelm Leibniz

This chapter delves into the historical evolution of computing, tracing its roots back to the 17th century with Blaise Pascal's invention of the Pascaline, a mechanical calculator. It highlights the endeavours of innovators such as Leibniz, Charles Babbage, and Joseph Marie Jacquard, each contributing to the development of calculating machines and the incorporation of punch card technology. The narrative progresses through the introduction of the Analytical Engine by Babbage, the punch card innovations inspired by Jacquard, and Herman Hollerith's electromechanical tabulating machine, which laid the foundation for IBM. Theoretical breakthroughs by Alan Turing and Alonzo Church on computability and the Church-Turing thesis are explored, emphasizing the inherent limits of computation. The chapter closes by recognizing Gordon Moore's observation in 1965, now famously known as Moore's Law, predicting the doubling of transistors in integrated circuits every two years, a phenomenon that has significantly shaped the trajectory of computing technology.

A Pascaline signed by Pascal in 1652. Image source: Wikipedia.

In 1642 the 18-year-old Blaise Pascal (1632-1662) was assisting his father, who worked as the supervisor of taxes in Rouen. The workload was considerable. Pascal was keen to simplify it. The idea of a calculator was born. The resulting machine, nicknamed the *Pascaline*, could add and subtract two numbers directly and perform multiplication and division through repeated addition or subtraction. In 1649, King Louis XIV of France gave Pascal a royal privilege, which provided the exclusive right to design and manufacture calculating machines in France.

Leibniz attempted to add automatic multiplication to the Pascaline and invented the *Leibniz wheels* in 1673. A century and a half later, in 1820, Thomas de Colmar (1875-1870) designed his *arithmometer*, the first mechanical calculator sturdy enough for daily office use. It is not clear whether he ever saw Leibniz's device, but he either re-invented it or utilized Leibniz's invention of the step drum.

The Pascaline, Leibniz wheels, and arithmometer worked on numbers and performed arithmetic. Modern computers spend much of their time processing text. Jonathan Swift (1667-1745) predicted text processing in his 1726 satirical novel *Gulliver's Travels*. We are all familiar with Lemuel Gulliver's voyages to Lilliput and Brobdingnag. On his less famous trip to Laputa he visited the Grand Academy at Lagado and met a learned gentleman who had devoted all his thoughts since his youth to what was undoubtedly a system of text processing, which Swift describes this:

The first professor I saw was in a very large room with forty pupils about him. After salutation, observing me to look earnestly upon a frame, which took up the greatest part of both the length and breadth of the room, he said perhaps I might wonder to see him employed in a project for improving speculative knowledge by practical and mechanical operations. But the world would soon be sensible of its usefulness, and he flattered himself that a more noble exalted thought never sprang in any other man's head. Every one knew how laborious the usual method is of attaining to arts and sciences; whereas, by his contrivance, the most ignorant person, at a reasonable charge, and with a little bodily labour, might write books in philosophy, poetry, politics, laws, mathematics, and theology, without the least assistance from genius or study. He then led me to the frame, about the sides, whereof all his pupils stood in ranks. It was twenty foot square, placed in the middle of the room. The superficies was composed of several bits of wood, about the bigness of a die, but some larger than others. They were all linked together by slender wires. These bits of wood were covered, on every square, with papers pasted on them; and on these papers were written all the words of their language, in their several moods, tenses, and declensions, but without any order. The professor then desired me to observe; for he was going to set his engine at work. The pupils at his command took each of them hold of an iron handle, whereof there were forty fixed round the edges of the frame, and giving them a sudden turn, the whole disposition of the words was entirely changed. He then commanded six-and-thirty of the lads, to read the several lines softly, as they appeared upon the frame; and where they found three or four words together that might make part of a sentence, they dictated to the four remaining boys, who were scribes. This work was repeated three or four times, and at every turn the engine was so contrived, that the words shifted into new places, as the square bits of wood moved upside down.

Jonathan Swift's Engine. Drawing by Theodore Ruoff.
Reproduced from *Computers and Law*, No. 12, May 1977-7.

Little did Swift know that in the 2010s representation learning and deep neural network-style machine learning would become widespread in natural language processing, and would achieve state-of-the-art results in many natural language tasks, for example in language modelling, parsing, and machine translation. This is increasingly important in medicine and healthcare, where NLP is being used to analyze notes and text in electronic health records that would otherwise be inaccessible for study when seeking to improve care.

Let's return to the 19th century. When it came to more complex calculations, machines were of limited use. Printed mathematical tables were calculated by human computers. They were central to navigation, science, and engineering.

In his memoirs, Charles Babbage (1791-1871) recalls:

My friend [John] Herschel calling upon me, brought with him the calculations of the [human] computers, and we commenced the tedious process of verification. After a time many discrepancies occured, and at one point these discordances were so numerous, that I exclaimed "I wish to God these calculations had been executed by steam", to which Herschel replied "It is quite possible."

Babbage conceived the idea of a *Difference Engine* for computing values of polynomial functions in 1822. In the next year he hired Joseph Clement to implement the design. Around 1831 Babbage and Clement fell out over the costs. Some parts of the prototype survive in the Museum of the History of Science in Oxford. Although Babbage received ample funding for the project, it was never completed.

Later (1847-1849) he produced detailed drawings for an improved version, "Difference Engine No. 2", but received no funding from the British government. His design was finally constructed posthumously in 1989-1991, using his plans and 19th-century manufacturing tolerances. It performed its first calculation at the Science Museum, London, returning results to 31 digits.

The Science Museum's Difference Engine No. 2, built from Babbage's design.

After the attempt at making the first Difference Engine fell through, Babbage worked to design a more complex machine called the *Analytical Engine*. He hired C. G. Jarvis, who had previously worked for Clement as a draughtsman. The Analytical Engine marks the transition from mechanized arithmetic to fully-fledged general-purpose computation. It is largely on it that Babbage's standing as computer pioneer rests.

In 1804, Joseph Marie Jacquard (1752-1834) invented a machine-controlled, programmable loom. It was controlled by punch cards laced together into a continuous sequence. Multiple rows of holes were punched on each card, with one complete card corresponding to one row of the design. This mechanism made possible the automatic production of unlimited varieties of pattern weaving. This portrait of Jacquard was woven in silk on a Jacquard loom and required 24,000 punched cards to create (1839). It was only produced to order. Babbage owned one of these portraits; it inspired him in using perforated cards in his Analytical Engine – a major computing innovation. The machine was also intended to employ several features subsequently used in modern computers, including sequential control, branching and looping. The Engine was not a single physical machine, but rather a succession of designs that Babbage tinkered with until his death in 1871.

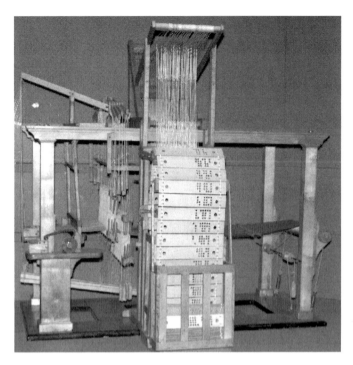

Jacquard's loom and punch cards. Image source: *Prostheses for the Brain*, 2021.

Jacquard's punch card idea was utilized in 1882 by the American inventor Herman Hollerith (1860-1929) in an electromechanical tabulating machine to assist in summarizing information and, later, in accounting. His invention marks the beginning of the era of mechanized binary code and semiautomatic data processing systems, and his concept dominated that landscape for nearly a century.

Hollerith founded a company that was amalgamated in 1911 with several other companies to form the Computing-Tabulating-Recording Company. In 1924, the company was renamed "International Business Machines" (IBM) and became one of the largest and most successful companies of the 20th century.

The English mathematician Alan Turing (1912-1954) approached the problem of computation from the theoretical side. While he was a fellow at Cambridge, he postulated an abstract *Turing machine*

(1936) that manipulates symbols on a strip of tape according to a table of rules. Despite the model's simplicity, given any computer algorithm, a Turing machine capable of simulating that algorithm's logic can be constructed. Independently, and around the same time, the American mathematician Alonzo Church postulated another mathematical model of computation – the *lambda calculus*.

Mathematical models of computation enabled Church and Turing to prove properties of computation in general. The *Entscheidungsproblem* ("decision problem") was posed by Hilbert and Wilhelm Ackermann (1896-1962) in 1928. It asked for an algorithm that considers, as input, a statement and answers "Yes" or "No" according to whether the statement is *universally valid*, i.e., valid in every structure satisfying the axioms. In 1936, Church and Turing published independent papers showing that a general solution to the *Entscheidungsproblem* is impossible, assuming that the intuitive notion of "effectively calculable" is captured by the functions computable by a Turing machine (or equivalently, by those expressible in the lambda calculus). This assumption is now known as the *Church-Turing thesis*.

Turing's work on the theory of computation led to the idea of a *computable number* – one for which there is a Turing machine which, given n on its initial tape, terminates with the nth digit of that number encoded on its tape. Not all real numbers are computable. For example, the probability that a random computer program will run forever, the so-called *Chaitin's constant*, named after Gregory Chaitin (b. 1947), is not computable.

Another fundamental limitation of computation was established by Turing. The *halting problem* is the problem of determining, from a description of an arbitrary computer program and an input, whether the program will finish running, or continue to run forever. Turing proved that a general algorithm to solve the halting problem for all possible program-input pairs cannot exist.

A system of data-manipulation rules (such as a computer's instruction set, a programming language, or a cellular automaton) is said to be *Turing-complete* or *computationally universal* if it can be used to simulate any Turing machine. Virtually all programming languages today are Turing-complete.

The American physicist and inventor John Vincent Atanasoff (1903-1995) attempted to build the first computer without gears, cams, belts, or shafts with the help of graduate student Clifford Berry (1918-1963). This attempt resulted in the *Atanasoff-Berry computer (ABC)*, the fist automatic electronic digital computer (1942). Limited by the technology of the day, and execution, the device has remained somewhat obscure. The ABC's priority is debated among historians of computer technology, because it was neither programmable, nor Turing-complete. Conventionally, the ABC would be considered the first electronic ALU (Arithmetic Logic Unit) – which is integrated into every modern processor's design. Its unique contribution was to make computing faster by being the first to use vacuum tubes to do the arithmetic calculations.

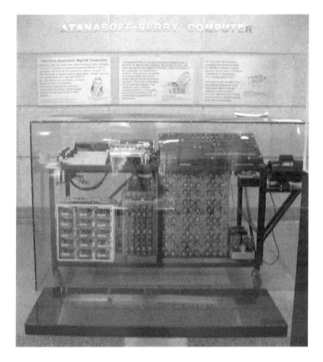

Atanasoff-Berry computer replica at Durham Center, Iowa State University.

Work on computers accelerated during the World War II. John Mauchly (1907-1980) and J. Presper Eckert (1919-1995) of the University of Pennsylvania developed *ENIAC (Electronic Numerical Integrator and Computer)* – the first programmable, electronic, general-purpose digital computer. It was Turing-complete and able to solve a large class of numerical problems through reprogramming. ENIAC was initially designed to calculate artillery firing tables for the U.S. Army's Ballistic Research Laboratory. However, its first program was a study of the feasibility of the thermonuclear weapon. Work on ENIAC commenced in 1943, it was completed in 1945, and first put to work for practical purposes on 10th December, 1945. T. R. Kennedy Jr. wrote in The New York Times on 15th February, 1946:

> One of the war's top secrets, an amazing machine which applies electronic speeds for the first time to mathematical tasks hitherto too difficult and cumbersome for solution, was announced here tonight by the War Department. Leaders who saw the device for the first time heralded it as a tool with which to begin to rebuild scientific affairs on new foundations.
>
> Such instruments, it was said, could revolutionize modern engineering, bring on a new epoch of industrial design, and eventually eliminate much slow and costly trial-and-error development work now deemed necessary in the fashioning of intricate machines. Heretofore, sheer mathematical difficulties have often forced designers to accept inferior solutions of their problems, with higher costs and slower progress.
>
> The "Eniac", as the new electronic speed marvel is known, virtually eliminates time in doing such jobs. Its inventors say it computes a mathematical problem 1,000 times faster than

62

it has ever been done before. The machine is being used on a problem in nuclear physics.

The Eniac, known more formally as "the electronic numerical integrator and computer," has not a single moving mechanical part. Nothing inside its 18,000 vacuum tubes and several miles of wiring moves except the tiniest elements of matter-electrons. There are, however, mechanical devices which translate or "interpret" the mathematical language of man to terms understood by the Eniac, and vice versa.

ENIAC programmers Frances Bilas (later Frances Spence) and Betty Jean Jennings (later Jean Bartik) stand at the main control panels of ENIAC. Both held degrees in mathematics. Bilas operated the Moore School's Differential Analyzer before joining the ENIAC project.

In 1944 Mauchly and Eckert started work on a new design, to be called the *EDVAC* (*Electronic Discrete Variable Automatic Computer*), which would be both simpler and more powerful. In particular, in 1944 Eckert wrote his description of a memory unit (the mercury delay line) which would hold both the data and the program. Unlike its predecessor, the ENIAC, EDVAC was binary rather than decimal, and was designed to be a stored-program computer. John von Neumann (1903-1957), who was consulting the University of Pennsylvania's Moore School of Electronic Engineering on the EDVAC, wrote up the *First Draft of a Report on the EDVAC*, which documented the design of a computer using the stored-program concept, which has come to be known as the *von Neumann architecture*.

In a stored-program computer the program instructions are stored electronically or optically accessible memory. This contrasts with systems that stored the program instructions with plugboards or similar mechanisms. Other features of the von Neumann architecture include:

- A processing unit that contains an arithmetic logic unit and processor registers.
- A control unit that contains an instruction register and program counter.
- Memory that stores data and instructions.
- External mass storage.
- Input and output mechanisms.

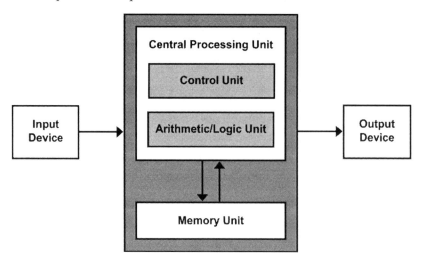

The von Neumann architecture.

Most modern computers have evolved from the von Neumann architecture.

In his *First Draft of a Report on the EDVAC* von Neumann cited the work on artificial neurons by Warren McCulloch and Walter Pitts. We will encounter their work in the chapter on the human brain and the perceptrons. It is interesting that artificial neurons served as an inspiration for the modern computer architecture. Later, in the 2010s, computer architecture (GPU as well as CPU) will serve as an enabler of deep learning.

Patsy Simmers, holding ENIAC board; Gail Taylor, holding EDVAC board; Milly Beck, holding ORDVAC board; and Norma Stec, holding BRLESC-I board.

In 1946 Mauchly and Eckert left the University of Pennsylvania and received funding from the Census Bureau to build the UNIVAC (Universal Automatic Computer), the first commercial computer for business and government applications.

In 1951 the UNIVAC I mainframe computer was built. It became known for predicting the outcome of the U.S. presidential election the following year. The computer predicted an Eisenhower landslide over Adlai Stevenson, whereas the final Gallup poll had

Eisenhower winning the popular vote 51-49 in a close contest. The prediction led CBS's news boss in New York, Sigfried Mickelson, to believe the computer was in error, and he refused to allow the prediction to be read. When the predictions proved true – Eisenhower defeated Stevenson in a landslide, with UNIVAC coming within 3.5% of his popular vote total and four votes of his Electoral College total – Charles Collingwood, the on-air announcer, announced that they had failed to believe the earlier prediction.

In 1947, William Shockley (1910-1989), John Bardeen (1908-1991, the only person to be awarded the Nobel Prize in Physics twice), and Walter Brattain (1902-1987) of Bell Laboratories invented the *transistor* – a semiconductor device used to amplify or switch electronic signals and electrical power with solid materials and no need for a vacuum. In 1958, Jack Kilby (1923-2005) and Robert Noyce (1927-1990) unveiled the integrated circuit, known as the computer chip. These inventions ushered in a new era in computing: computers would become much faster, smaller, and cheaper.

In 1964 Douglas Engelbart (1925-2013) showed a prototype of the modern computer, with a mouse and a graphical user interface (GUI). This marked the evolution of the computer from a specialized machine for scientists and mathematicians to technology that is more accessible to the general public.

The latter half of the 20th century saw rapid adoption and proliferation of digital computers and digital record-keeping, a trend that continues to the present day. This trend is known as the *Digital Revolution* or the *Third Industrial Revolution*. It constitutes a shift from mechanical and analogue electronic technology to digital electronics. The figure below, reproduced from Wikipedia, shows some important dates in Digital Revolution from 1968 to 2017 as rings of time on a tree:

In 1965 Gordon Moore (b. 1929), the co-founder of Fairchild Semiconductor and Intel (and former CEO of the latter) observed a doubling every year in the number of components per integrated circuit, and projected this rate of growth would continue for at least another decade. In 1975, looking forward to the next decade, he revised the forecast to doubling every two years. His prediction held since 1975 and has since become known as a "law". The modern statement of *Moore's law* is that the number of transistors in a dense integrated circuit doubles about every two years.

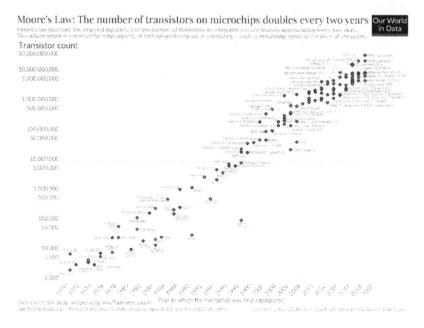

A semi-log plot of transistor counts for microprocessors against dates of introduction, nearly doubling every two years.

As economist Richard G. Anderson notes,

> Numerous studies have traced the cause of the productivity acceleration to technological innovations in the production of semiconductors that sharply reduced the prices of such components and of the products that contain them (as well as expanding the capabilities of such products).

Chapter 5: Programming languages

> It seems that perfection is attained, not when there is nothing more to add, but when there is nothing more to take away.
>
> Antoine de Saint Exupéry

In this chapter, Emanuel Derman, an expert programmer, offers insights into the creative and complex nature of programming, drawing parallels with poetry and music. The collaborative aspect of programming is emphasized, highlighting the need for effective communication through code within teams. The chapter explores the historical development of programming languages, from early specialized languages with obscure syntax to the advent of high-level languages like Plankalkül, FORTRAN, and the revolutionary C language. Object-oriented programming (OOP) and its impact on software complexity are discussed, leading to the evolution of languages like C++, Java, and C#. The narrative then delves into the success of Python, particularly in the field of artificial intelligence (AI), and the emergence of key libraries like scikit-learn, TensorFlow, PyTorch, and Keras that have played pivotal roles in making AI accessible. The chapter underscores the importance of programming talent, creativity, and experience, and the open-source revolution's role in bringing AI to a broader audience.

An expert *programmer* (or *coder*) Emanuel Derman (b. 1945) explains what it's like to program in his memoir:

> What are you doing when you program? You are trying to use a language to specify an imagined world and its details as accurately as possible. You are trying to create this world on a machine that can understand and execute only simple

commands. You do this solely by writing precise instructions, often many hundreds of lines long. Your sequence of instructions must be executed without ambiguity, by an uncomprehending automaton, the computer, and yet, in parallel, must be read, comprehended, remembered and modified by you and other programmers. Just as poetry strives to resolve the tension between form and meaning, so programming must resolve the conflict between intelligibility and concision. In this endeavor, the language you employ is critically important.

The comparison with poetry is not accidental. Programming is a very creative endeavour. To the American cognitive and computer scientist Marvin Minsky (1927-2016) programming is more akin to playing music:

> A computer is like a violin. You can imagine a novice trying first a phonograph and then a violin. The latter, he says, sounds terrible. That is the argument we have heard from our humanists and most of our computer scientists. Computer programs are good, they say, for particular purposes, but they aren't flexible. Neither is violin, or a typewriter, until you learn how to use it.

Programmers don't work in isolation; programming usually requires group effort. Like the ancient guilds of cathedral builders, they work in teams and must communicate with each other, and they communicate through code. Harold Abelson (b. 1947) and Gerald Jay Sussman (b. 1947) explain:

> ...programs must be written for people to read and only incidentally for machines to execute.

The Dutch programmer and the creator of the programming language Python, Guido van Rossum (b. 1956), seconds:

> You primarily write your code to communicate with other coders, and, to a lesser extent, to impose your will on the computer.

This is particularly true of artificial intelligence (AI) programming. AI is complex. A successful AI application is built on hundreds, perhaps thousands, of experiments. These experiments must be programmed, and are usually programmed by teams of data scientists, rather than by a single person. Grady Booch:

> The task of the software development team is to create an illusion of simplicity. We build abstractions to help us create this illusion; these abstractions are an essential way we mitigate the intellectual complexity that lurks within our systems…

Ada Lovelace (1815-1852), who corresponded with Babbage during his development of the Analytical Engine, is credited with developing an algorithm that would enable the Engine to calculate a sequence of Bernoulli numbers. For this achievement, she is often described as the first computer programmer; though no programming language had yet been invented.

Early programming languages were highly specialized and had obscure, incomprehensible syntax. Before high-level programming languages were invented, programmers wrote hand-tuned assembly language programs. The *assembly* is only slightly removed from the "metal" (the hardware); it is a low-level programming language. It was eventually realized that programming in assembly required a great deal of intellectual effort. Peter Norton (b. 1943), who wrote several textbooks on assembly, would later say

> Assembly language programming is an extravagant waste of not only human talent and should be avoided whenever possible.

The following assembly program prints "Hello, world!" on the screen:

```
section .text

    global  _start

_start:
```

```
        mov     edx,len
        mov     ecx,msg
        mov     ebx,1
        mov     eax,4
        int     0x80
        mov     ebx,0
        mov     eax,1
        int     0x80

section .data

msg db      "Hello, World!",0xa
len equ     $ - msg
```

The first high-level programming language was Plankalkül, created by Konrad Zuse (1910-1995) between 1942 and 1945. The first high-level language to have an associated compiler[1] was created by Corrado Böhm (1923-2017) in 1951, for his PhD thesis. The first commercially available language was FORTRAN (FORmula TRANslation) developed in 1954 by a team led by John Backus (1924-2007) at IBM. John Backus explained,

> Much of my work has come from being lazy. I didn't like writing programs, and so, when I was working on the IBM 701 (an early computer), writing programs for computing missile trajectories, I started work on a programming system to make it easier to write programs.

When FORTRAN was first introduced, it was viewed with scepticism due to bugs, delays in development, and the comparative efficiency of "hand-coded" programs written in assembly. However, in a hardware market that was rapidly evolving, the language eventually became known for its efficiency.

Here is an equivalent of the above "Hello, World!" program in FORTRAN:

---

[1] A *compiler* is a computer program that translates computer code written in one language (typically a high-level language) into another language (typically a lower-level language, such as assembly).

72

```
program hello
  print *, 'Hello, World!'
end program hello
```

The operating system Unix was developed in the mid-1960s by Ken Thompson (b. 1943), Dennis Ritchie (1941-2011), Brian Kernighan (b. 1942), Douglas McIlroy (b. 1932), and Joe Ossanna (1928-1977) at Bell Labs. Thompson desired a programming language to make utilities for the new platform. At first, he tried to make a FORTRAN compiler, but soon gave up the idea. Instead, he created a cut-down version of the recently developed BCPL systems programming language. The official description of BCPL was not available at the time, and Thompson modified the syntax to be less wordy, producing the similar but somewhat simpler B. However, few utilities were ultimately written in B because it was too slow, and B could not take advantage of PDP-11 features such as byte addressability.

In 1972, Ritchie started to improve B, which resulted in creating a new language C. The C compiler and some utilities made with it were included in Version 2 Unix. At version 4 Unix, released in November 1973, the Unix kernel was extensively reimplemented in C. By this time, the C language had acquired some powerful features such as struct types.

Programmers started migrating from FORTRAN to C. Derman recalls:

> ...at AT&T in 1980, the whole firm was embracing C, the simultaneously graceful and yet practical language invented by Dennis Ritchie about ten years earlier at Murray Hill. He had devised C to be a high-level tool with which to write portable versions of UNIX, the operating system also invented there by Ken Thompson and Ritchie. Now everything from telephone switching systems to word-processing software was being written in C, on UNIX, all with amazing style. Eventually, even physicists, who are generally interested only in the number of digits after a decimal point, began to forsake ugly utilitarian FORTRAN

for poetically stylish C. Programming was in the late stages of a revolution about which I was just beginning to learn.

Simula was developed by Ole-Johan Dahl (1931-2002) and Kirsten Nygaard (1926-2002) at the Norwegian Computing Center in Oslo. The language introduced the initial ideas of *object-oriented programming (OOP)*, a programming paradigm based on the concept of *objects*, which can contain data and code. In 1985 Bjarne Stroustrup (b. 1950) created C++ inheriting most of C's syntax and introducing the OOP ideas from Simula to obtain "a light-weight abstraction programming language [designed] for building and using efficient and elegant abstractions". Stroustrup explains that "offering both hardware access and abstraction is the basis of C++. Doing it efficiently is what distinguishes it from other languages." These innovations enabled the construction of large, complex software projects consisting of numerous interoperating components. Later languages, such as Java (1995, designed by James Gosling) and C# (2000, designed by Anders Hejlsberg) followed in the C++ tradition.

The invention of OOP enabled programmers to decompose a complicated work based on objects rather than functions. This decomposition made it possible to build highly complex software. Objects corresponded more closely to real-world entities than the earlier *functions*. Through *inheritance*, it is possible to utilize the features of an existing class of objects in a new class without repeating the existing code. Inheritance minimizes complexity. Since, in the words of Bruce Eckel (b. 1957), "programming is about managing complexity: the complexity of the problem, laid upon the complexity of the machine", OOP, which achieved a reduction in complexity, significantly simplified the programming challenge.

But, while OOP does facilitate the creation of complex software systems, it is important to remember that OOP is not a "silver bullet" (a term made popular by Fred Brooks (b. 1931)). Programming a computer is still one of the most difficult tasks ever undertaken by humankind; becoming proficient in programming requires talent, creativity, intelligence, logic, the ability to build and

74

use abstractions, and experience – even when the best of tools are available.

In 1991 van Rossum released the first version of another programming language, Python. It supported many of the features of its predecessors, such as the support for object-oriented programming found in C++, Java, and C#. The language's core philosophy is summarized in the document *The Zen of Python* (*PEP 20*), which includes aphorisms such as:

- Beautiful is better than ugly.
- Explicit is better than implicit.
- Simple is better than complex.
- Complex is better than complicated.
- Readability counts.

Our "Hello, World!" example becomes a single line in Python:

```
print('Hello, World!')
```

A programming language is more than its syntax and semantics. C++, Java, and C# have established entire ecosystems of dedicated fans and supporting software. This supporting software consists of programming tools and software *libraries* – suites of programming code used to develop other software programs and applications. There are libraries for logging the state of the programs, for networking, for working with data and, increasingly, for AI. Python has been particularly successful in creating a following among AI experts. Van Rossum explains:

> The currently prevailing theory about Python's unexpected success is that at some point, it established itself into data science and machine learning, and scientific data processing in general, and once you have critical mass, it's easier for everyone to use the same system as their colleagues and their competitors, than to try something different.

Python has become the *lingua franca* of artificial intelligence.

In 2007 David Cournapeau released scikit-learn, a Python library for machine learning. A few years later came the software library TensorFlow, which was published by the Google Brain Team in 2015. In 2016, Facebook's AI Research lab (FAIR) published its own library for building neural networks, PyTorch. Keras, developed by François Chollet, a Google engineer, greatly simplified the creation and operation of neural networks in TensorFlow.

These libraries are *free and open-source software (FOSS)*, meaning that anyone is freely licensed to use, copy, study, and change the software in any way, and the source code is openly shared so that people are encouraged to voluntarily improve the design of the software. The open-source revolution pioneered by Richard Stallman (b. 1953) and other activists has been instrumental in bringing artificial intelligence to the masses. Implementing your own neural network system is a highly nontrivial matter. TensorFlow, Keras, and PyTorch make this task straightforward.

Chapter 6: Cybernetics

> In control and communication we are always fighting nature's tendency to degrade the organized and to destroy the meaningful; the tendency, as Gibbs has shown us, for entropy to increase.
>
> Norbert Wiener

The chapter explores the evolution and impact of cybernetics, tracing its origins to Norbert Wiener's seminal work in 1948. Cybernetics, coined from the Greek term for "steersman," aimed to unify the study of communication, control, and statistical mechanics in both machines and living organisms. Initially focused on behavioristic approaches and purposeful concepts, cybernetics soon expanded beyond its foundational principles. The narrative highlights cybernetics' contributions to robotics and control systems, emphasizing the significance of feedback loops and communication in designing autonomous machines. As artificial intelligence (AI) emerged, cybernetic ideas influenced machine learning algorithms, transforming AI capabilities in areas such as smart assistants and predictive analytics. Despite success, cybernetics faces challenges, including oversimplified portrayals of automata and ethical concerns. The chapter concludes by discussing the resurgence of cybernetics in interdisciplinary collaborations, integrating principles with quantum computing and bioinformatics, showcasing its enduring relevance in shaping our understanding and application of information processing, control, and communication.

The American mathematician Norbert Wiener (1894-1964) wasn't content with the progress made by computing in his day. In 1948 he published the book *Cybernetics: Or Control and Communication in the Animal and the Machine.*

In his book, Wiener describes the origins of cybernetics:

Thus, as far back as four years ago, the group of scientists about [Dr. Arturo Rosenblueth (1900-1970)] and myself had already become aware of the essential unity of the set of problems centering about communication, control, and statistical mechanics, whether in the machine or in living tissue. On the other hand, we were seriously hampered by the lack of unity of the literature concerning these problems, and by the absence of any common terminology, or even of a single name for the field. After much consideration, we have come to the conclusion that all of the existing terminology was too heavy a bias to one side or another to serve the future development of the field as well as it should; and as happens so often to scientists, we have been forced to coin at least one artificial neo-Greek expression to fill the gap. We have decided to call the entire field of control and communication theory, whether in the machine or in the animal, by the name *Cybernetics*, which we form from the Greek κυβερνήτης or *steersman*. In choosing this term, we wish to recognize that the first significant paper on feedback mechanisms is an article on governors, which was published by Clerk Maxwell in 1868, and that *governor* is derived from a Latin corruption of κυβερνήτης. We also wish to refer to the fact that steering engines of a ship are indeed one of the earliest and best-developed forms of feedback mechanisms.

Many ideas of cybernetics can be traced back to the essay *Behavior, Purpose and Teleology* (1943) by Rosenblueth, Wiener, and Julian Bigelow (1913-2003). The authors had set for themselves two goals:

(1) to define the behaviouristic study of natural events and to classify behaviour;
(2) to stress the importance of the concept of purpose.

The *behaviouristic approach* consists in the examination of the *output* of an object (an animal, a machine) and of the relations of this output to the *input*. By output is meant any change produced in the surroundings by the object. By input, any event external to the object that modifies this object in any manner.

This approach is contrasted to the alternative *functional* method of study, which is concerned with the intrinsic organization of the entity studied, its structure and its properties; the relations between the object and the surroundings are relatively incidental.

By *behaviour* is meant any change of an entity with respect to its surroundings. This change may be largely an output from the object, the input being then minimal, remote, or irrelevant; or else the change may be immediately traceable to a certain input. Accordingly, any modification of an object detectable externally, may be denoted as behaviour. The term would be, therefore, too extensive for usefulness were it not that it may be restricted by apposite adjectives – i.e., that behaviour may be classified.

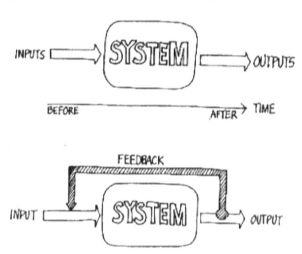

I belong to those extremely desperate cyberneticians who do not see any significant limitations in the cybernetic approach to the problem of life and believe that it is possible to analyze life in all its fullness, including human consciousness with all its complexity, using the methods of cybernetics.

In a letter to A.I. Berg, Kolmogorov wrote:

> One should, however, understand that the real successes of cybernetics and automation on this path are significantly more modest than they are sometimes portrayed to be in popular books and articles. When describing "self-learning" automata or automata capable of "composing" musing or writing poetry, one sometimes assumes an overly simplified idea of the nature of the human higher nervous activity, in particular, of human creativity.

Steven Strogatz, in *Sync*, stated that

> every decade or so, a grandiose theory comes along bearing similar aspirations and often brandishing an ominous-sounding C-name. In the 1960s it was cybernetics. In the 1970s it was catastrophe theory. Then came chaos theory in the '80s and complexity theory in the '90s.

As cybernetics took its initial steps with the pioneering work of Norbert Wiener and his colleagues, it quickly evolved beyond its foundational principles. In the subsequent years, cybernetics found widespread applications in various fields, showcasing its adaptability and versatility.

One significant domain where cybernetics has left an indelible mark is in the realm of robotics and control systems. The principles of feedback loops and communication, central to cybernetics, have been instrumental in designing autonomous robotic systems. From industrial automation to the development of robotic prosthetics, cybernetic approaches have contributed to the advancement of intelligent, self-regulating machines.

As artificial intelligence (AI) emerged as a prominent field, cybernetic concepts became integral to AI systems. Machine learning algorithms, inspired by cybernetic ideas of learning from feedback, have revolutionized the capabilities of AI. Today's smart assistants, recommendation systems, and predictive analytics owe their efficiency to the principles first articulated in cybernetics.

Despite its successes, cybernetics has faced its share of challenges and criticisms. As A.I. Berg aptly pointed out, the portrayal of "self-learning" automata and creative machines sometimes oversimplifies the intricacies of human higher nervous activity. The dream of machines composing music or writing poetry is a complex endeavour that goes beyond the initial aspirations of cybernetics.

Additionally, ethical concerns and questions about the potential unintended consequences of implementing cybernetic systems have surfaced. Issues related to privacy, bias in decision-making, and the societal impact of highly autonomous systems are part of the ongoing discourse within the field.

In recent years, cybernetics has experienced a resurgence, fuelled by advancements in computing power, data availability, and interdisciplinary collaborations. Researchers are exploring new frontiers, integrating cybernetic principles with emerging technologies such as quantum computing and bioinformatics.

Steven Strogatz's observation about grandiose theories, including cybernetics, prompts a reflection on how cybernetics compares to subsequent theories like catastrophe theory, chaos theory, and complexity theory. Each theory brings unique perspectives, with cybernetics focusing on feedback and communication, chaos theory on nonlinear dynamics, and complexity theory on the emergent behaviour of complex systems.

To illustrate the tangible impact of cybernetics, consider the case of autonomous vehicles. These vehicles employ cybernetic principles for real-time decision-making based on feedback from sensors, navigating complex environments with a level of autonomy that was once considered futuristic.

Another example is the field of neuroprosthetics, where cybernetic concepts are applied to create brain-machine interfaces, enabling individuals with paralysis to control robotic limbs through neural signals.

In conclusion, cybernetics has transitioned from its early theoretical foundations to become a driving force behind innovations in robotics, AI, and various interdisciplinary fields. It has weathered criticisms and challenges, adapting to the evolving landscape of technology and human understanding. As we move forward, the principles of cybernetics continue to shape our endeavours to understand and harness the complexities of information processing, control, and communication in both machines and living organisms.

Chapter 7: The human brain and perceptrons

> If the human brain were so simple that we could understand it, we would be so simple that we couldn't.
>
> Emerson M. Pugh

The chapter delves into the intricacies of the human brain, highlighting its role as the central command center of the nervous system. Four main regions, including the cerebrum, cerebellum, brainstem, and diencephalon, collaborate to ensure the organism's optimal functioning. The cerebrum, the largest part, encompasses the cerebral cortex and subcortical structures, crucial for sensory processing and perception. Various lobes of the cerebral cortex handle functions like speech, language, and motor skills. The hippocampus aids in processing declarative and spatial memories, while procedural memory involves the basal ganglia, cerebellum, and supplementary motor cortex. The chapter touches on the brain's remarkable ability to remember, which starts in the womb, and the anatomical structure of neurons, the fundamental units of the nervous system.

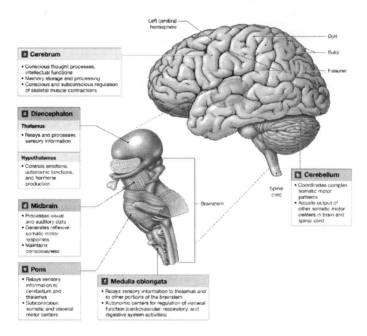

The *human brain* is the command centre of the human nervous system. It receives signals from the body's sensory organs and outputs information to the muscles. The brain consists of four main regions – the cerebrum, the cerebellum, the brainstem, and the diencephalon. They function as a whole to ensure that the organism is operational.

The *cerebrum* is the largest part of the brain containing the *cerebral cortex*, as well as several subcortical structures, including the *hippocampus*, *basal ganglia*, and *olfactory bulb*. The lobes of the cerebral cortex include the *frontal*, *temporal*, *occipital*, and *parietal*.

The cerebrum is made up of the approximately symmetric left and right *cerebral hemispheres* and their cerebral cortices (the outer layer of *grey matter*), and the underlying regions of *white matter*.

The primary sensory areas of the cerebral cortex receive and process visual (images), auditory (sounds), somatosensory (pressure, pain, warmth), gustatory (taste), and olfactory (smell) information. These brain regions synthesize sensory information into our perceptions of the world.

Speech and language are mainly attributed to parts of the cerebral cortex. Motor portions of language are attributed to *Broca's area* within the frontal lobe. Speech comprehension is attributed to *Wernicke's area*, at the temporal-parietal lobe junction. These two regions are interconnected by a large white matter tract, the *arcuate fasciculus*.

The hippocampus helps humans process and retrieve declarative memories and spatial relationships. *Declarative memories* are those related to facts and events, for examples lines in a play. *Spatial relationship memories* involve pathways or routes. For example, when a cab driver uses spatial memory to learn a route through a city. *Procedural memory* is defined as the ability to acquire cognitive and behavioural skills, which subsequently become automatic. For example, procedural memory is used to store the sequence of button pushes on a television remote to access a favourite program. This subtype of memory involves the basal ganglia, cerebellum, and supplementary motor cortex areas. Short-term or *working memory* involves association areas of the cortex, especially the dorsolateral prefrontal cortex, as well as the hippocampus.

Motor and Sensory Regions of the Cerebral Cortex

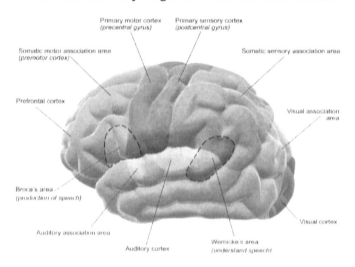

Research has shown that the brain starts remembering things from the womb. It stops growing when one is around 25, but that doesn't mean that an intellectual peak has been reached.

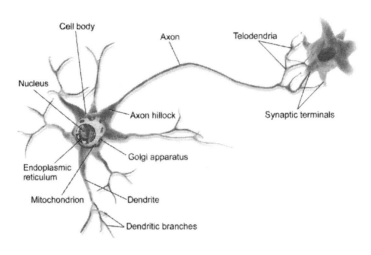

Anatomy of a multipolar neuron.

There are approximately 86 billion neurons in the human brain. A *neuron* is an electrically excitable cell that communicates with other cells via specialized connections called *synapses*. It is the main component of the nervous tissue.

A typical neuron consists of a cell body (*soma*), *dendrites*, and a single *axon*. The soma is usually compact. The axon and dendrites are filaments that extrude from it. Dendrites typically branch profusely and extend a few hundred micrometres from the soma. The axon leaves the soma at a swelling called the *axon hillock*, and travels for as far as one metre in humans or more in other species. It branches but usually maintains a constant diameter. At the farthest tip of the axon's branches are *axon terminals*, where the neuron can transmit a signal across the synapse to another cell.

Most neurons receive signals via the dendrites and soma and send out signals down the axon. At the majority of synapses, signals cross from the axon of one neuron to a dendrite of another.

However, synapses can connect an axon to another axon or a dendrite to another dendrite.

The signalling process is partly electrical and partly chemical. Neurons are electrically excitable, due to maintenance of voltage gradients across their membranes. If the voltage changes by a large enough amount over a short interval, the neuron generates an all-or-nothing electrochemical pulse called an action potential. This potential travels rapidly along the axon, and activates synaptic connections as it reaches them. Synaptic signals may be excitatory or inhibitory, increasing or reducing the net voltage that reaches the soma.

The neuron's place as the primary functional unit of the nervous system was first recognized in the late 19th century through the work of the Spanish anatomist Santiago Ramón y Cajal (1852-1934). To make the structure of individual neurons visible, Ramón y Cajal improved a silver staining process that had been developed by the Italian biologist Camillo Golgi (1843-1926). The improved process involves a technique called "double impregnation" and is still in use.

In 1888 Ramón y Cajal published a paper about the bird cerebellum. In this paper, he stated that he could not find evidence for anastomosis between axons and dendrites and called each nervous element "an absolutely autonomous canton." This became known as the *neuron doctrine*, one of the central tenets of modern neuroscience.

In 1891, the German anatomist Heinrich Wilhelm Waldeyer (1836-1921) wrote a highly influential review of the neuron doctrine in which he introduced the term *neuron* to describe the anatomical and physiological unit of the nervous system.

The Canadian psychologist Donald Hebb (1904-1985) sought to understand how the function of neurons contributed to psychological processes such as learning. He theorized that learning is a purely local phenomenon expressible in terms of synaptic change. Specifically, the synaptic change depends on both presynaptic and postsynaptic activities such that

> When an axon of cell *A* is near enough to excite a cell *B* and repeatedly or persistently takes part in firing it, some growth process or metabolic change takes place in one or both cells such that *A*'s efficiency as one of the cells firing *B*, is increased.

Hebb's learning rule states that the change in synaptic strength is a function of the temporal correlation between presynaptic and postsynaptic activities. Specifically, the synaptic strength between two neurons *A* and *B* increases whenever the two neurons are in the same state and decreases when they are in different states. In brief:

> With Hebbian learning, the connection between two neurons is proportional to the (temporal) correlation of their values during learning.

The first artificial neuron was the Threshold Logic Unit (TLU), or Linear Threshold Unit, first proposed by the American neurophysiologist Warren McCulloch (1898-1969) and the American logician Walter Pitts (1923-1969) in 1943.

The following article appeared in The New York Times on Tuesday, 8 July, 1958:

NEW NAVY DEVICE LEARNS BY DOING

Psychologist Shows Embryo of Computer Designed to Read and Grow Wiser

WASHINGTON, July 7 (UPI) – The Navy revealed the embryo of an electronic computer today that it expects will be able to walk, talk, see, write, reproduce itself and be conscious of its existence.

The embryo – the Weather Bureau's $2,000,000 "704" computer – learned to differentiate between right and left after fifty attempts in the Navy's demonstration for newsmen.

[...]

Dr. Rosenblatt said he could explain why the machine learned only in highly technical terms. But he said the computer had undergone a "self-induced change in the wiring diagram."

The first Perceptron will have about 1,000 electronic "association cells" receiving electrical impulses from an eye-like scanning device with 400 photo-cells. The human brain has 10,000,000,000 responsive cells, including 100,000,000 connections with the eyes.

Working on pattern classification, Frank Rosenblatt (1928 – 1971) of the Cornell Aeronautical Laboratory invented the **perceptron**. It was first implemented on IBM 704 and then as a custom-built machine, the Mark I Perceptron. That machine had an array of 400 photoresistors, randomly connected to the "neurons". The weights were encoded in potentiometers and weight updates were carried out by electric motors.

The Mark I Perceptron on exhibition at the National Museum of History and Technology, March 1968.

According to the manual,

> The Mark I Perceptron is a pattern learning and recognition device. It can learn to classify plane patterns into groups on the basis of certain geometric similarities and differences. Among the properties which it may use in its discriminations and generalizations are position in the retinal field of view, geometric form, occurrence frequency, and size.

> If, of the many possible bases of classification, a particular one is desired, it can generally be transferred to the perceptron by a forced learning session or by an error correction training process. If left to its own resources the perceptron can still divide up into classes the patterns presented to it, on a classification basis of its own forming. This formation process is commonly referred to as spontaneous learning.

> The Mark I is intended as an experimental tool for the direct study of a limited class of perceptrons. It is sufficiently flexible in configuration and operation to serve as a model for any of a large number of perceptrons possessing a single layer of non-cross-coupled association units.

Around the same time another early feedforward neural network algorithm was produced by Bernard Widrow and his first PhD student, Ted Hoff: the least mean squares (LMS) algorithm, also known as the Widrow-Hoff rule.

In the next year, 1961, Widrow and his students developed the earliest learning rule for feedforward networks with multiple adaptive elements: the Madaline Rule I (MRI).

Applications of LMS and MRI were developed by Widrow and his students in fields such as pattern recognition, weather forecasting, adaptive control, and signal processing. The work by R. W. Lucky and others at Bell laboratories led to first applications to adaptive equalization in high-speed modems and adaptive echo cancellers for long-distance telephone and satellite circuits.

Whereas the importance of neural networks in human decision making has been understood for a long time, researchers have discovered that the process of making decisions involves a complex interplay of various brain regions, and it's challenging to pinpoint a single area responsible for decision-making. However, the prefrontal cortex, particularly the dorsolateral prefrontal cortex (DLPFC), is often associated with higher-order cognitive functions, including decision-making.

The DLPFC is involved in tasks that require executive functions, such as working memory, cognitive flexibility, and the evaluation of potential outcomes. Studies using neuroimaging techniques, such as functional magnetic resonance imaging (fMRI), have shown increased activity in the DLPFC during decision-making processes.

Additionally, the orbitofrontal cortex (OFC), another region in the frontal lobes, is implicated in decision-making, particularly in evaluating rewards and punishments associated with different choices. The interaction between these prefrontal regions, along with other brain areas like the striatum and amygdala, contributes to the complex process of decision-making.

It is understood that decision-making is a dynamic and distributed process involving multiple brain regions working together rather than a single area solely responsible for this function. Different decisions and contexts may engage various neural circuits, adding to the complexity of understanding the neural basis of decision-making.

Chapter 8: Early AI

> Artificial intelligence is the science of making machines do things that would require intelligence if done by men.
>
> Marvin Minsky

The chapter explores the birth of artificial intelligence (AI) through a pivotal workshop in the summer of 1956 at Dartmouth College, led by John McCarthy, who coined the term "artificial intelligence." Attendees, including Marvin Minsky, Claude Shannon, and Herbert Simon, embarked on an ambitious goal of simulating every aspect of human learning and intelligence using machines. The narrative then delves into the contrasting approaches within AI, with McCarthy advocating for formal logic, leading to the creation of LISP, while Minsky, along with Seymour Papert, championed a more experimental "scruffy" approach. The chapter touches on significant developments, such as Terry Winograd's SHRDLU, a natural language understanding program, and the XOR affair, where Minsky's work with perceptrons was both praised and criticized, contributing to a decline in neural networks research. Despite the challenges, exceptions like Stephen Grossberg's Adaptive Resonance Theory and Teuvo Kohonen's work persisted, signifying the complex history and dynamics within the field of artificial intelligence.

In summer of 1956 a group of researchers gathered at a workshop organized by John McCarthy, then a young Assistant Professor of Mathematics, at Dartmouth College in Hanover, New Hampshire.

The attendees included:

- Marvin Minsky (1927-2016)
- Trenchard More (b. 1930)
- Nathaniel Rochester (1919-2001)

- Oliver Selfridge (1926-2008)
- Claude Shannon (1916-2001)
- Herbert Simon (1916-2001)
- Ray Solomonoff (1926-2009)

The stated goal was ambitious:

> The study is to proceed on the basis of the conjecture that every aspect of learning or any other feature of intelligence can, in principle, be so precisely described that a machine can be made to simulate it. An attempt will be made to find how to make machines use language, form abstractions and concepts, solve kinds of problems now reserved for humans, and improve themselves.

Thus, the field of artificial intelligence (AI) was born.

It was John McCarthy who coined the term artificial intelligence, which he defined as

the science and engineering of making intelligent machines, especially intelligent computer programs.

Here we see him hosting a series of four simultaneous computer chess matches carried out via telegraph against rivals in Russia ten years later, in 1966. (MIT archive photos.)

Marvin Minsky was born in New York City in 1927. He joined the MIT faculty in 1958 and stayed there until his death. He started at the MIT Lincoln Laboratory and then, jointly with John McCarthy, initiated what is, as of 2019, named the MIT Computer Science and

Artificial Intelligence Laboratory. Minsky worked closely with Seymour Papert (1928 – 2016), a South African-born mathematician, computer scientist, and educator, on what became known as th "scruffy" approach to AI. Minsky, Papert, and their colleagues did whatever it took to just get systems to do interesting things. Their students worked on problems in limited domains, application areas not requiring a broad general knowledge, such as integral calculus, geometry, algebra, as well as a famous series of problems in the "blocks world", a simplified world consisting of some toy blocks sitting on a table.

Terry Winograd (b. 1946) was at the time a PhD student of Seymour Papert. In 1968-70 he wrote SHRDLU[2], a program for understanding natural language. It conducted a simple dialog (via teletype) with a user about a blocks world shown on an early display screen (DEC-340 attached to a PDP-6 computer).

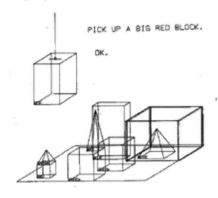

Ever wondered how SHRDLU got its name?

Here is an example dialogue that was used as a SHRDLU demo:

Person: PICK UP A BIG RED BLOCK.

Computer: OK. (does it)

Person: GRASP THE PYRAMID.

Computer: I DON'T UNDERSTAND WHICH PYRAMID YOU MEAN.

Person: FIND A BLOCK WHICH IS TALLER THAN THE ONE YOU ARE HOLDING AND PUT IT INTO THE BOX.

Computer: BY "IT", I ASSUME YOU MEAN THE BLOCK WHICH IS TALLER THAN THE ONE I AM HOLDING.

---

[2] Ever wondered how SHRDLU got its name? See this peace of AI history: https://hci.stanford.edu/winograd/shrdlu/name.html

Computer: OK. (does it)

Person: WHAT DOES THE BOX CONTAIN?

Computer: THE BLUE PYRAMID AND THE BLUE BLOCK.

Person: WHAT IS THE PYRAMID SUPPORTED BY?

Computer: THE BOX.

Person: HOW MANY BLOCKS ARE NOT IN THE BOX?

Computer: FOUR OF THEM.

Person: IS AT LEAST ONE OF THEM NARROWER THAN THE ONE WHICH I TOLD YOU TO PICK UP?

Computer: YES, THE RED CUBE.

Person: IS IT SUPPORTED?

Computer: YES, BY THE TABLE.

Person: CAN THE TABLE PICK UP BLOCKS?

Computer: NO.

Person: CAN A PYRAMID BE SUPPORTED BY A BLOCK?

Computer: YES.

. . .

Their work was not all about simulation. Here Minsky is pictured with a physical system consisting of a video camera and a robotic arm used to manipulate a physical blocks world.

John McCarthy, who came to MIT around the same time as Minsky, disliked the "scruffy" approach. He advocated the use of formal logic in artificial intelligence. He invented LISP, and co-developed it with R. Brayton, D. Edwards, P. Fox, L. Hodes, D. Luckham, K. Maling, D. Park, and S. Russell:

> A programming system called LISP (for LISt Processor) has been developed for the IBM 704 computer by the Artificial Intelligence group at M.I.T. The system was designed to facilitate experiments with a proposed system called the Advice Taker, whereby a machine could be instructed to handle declarative as well as imperative sentences and could exhibit "common sense" in carrying out its instructions. The original proposal for the Advice Taker was made in November 1958. The main requirement was a programming system for manipulating expressions representing formalized declarative and imperative sentences so that the Advice Taker system could make deductions.
>
> In the course of its development, the LISP system went through several stages of simplification and eventually came to be based on a scheme for representing the partial recursive functions of a certain class of symbolic expressions.

McCarthy's work was influenced by that of Allen Newell, J. Cliff Shaw, and Herber A. Simon on Logic Theorist, "the first artificial intelligence program", which would eventually prove 38 of the first 52 theorems in Alfred North Whitehead's and Betrand Russell's *Principia Mathematica* (not to be confused with Newton's eponymous work).

Minsky was critical of the use of logic for representing knowledge. In *Criticism of the Logistic Approach*, Minsky wrote:

Because logicians are not concerned with systems that will later be enlarged, they can design axioms that permit only the conclusions they want. In the development of intelligence, the situation is different. One has to learn which features of situations are important, and which kinds of deductions are not to be regarded seriously.

Thus, McCarthy's approach diverged from Minsky's and in 1963 McCarthy left MIT to start the Stanford Artificial Intelligence Laboratory.

As an alternative to formal logic, Minsky advocated an approach based on the so-called frames. Minsky's approach wasn't without its critics either, but Minsky's frames paper served to place knowledge representation as a central issue for AI.

During a 1958 press conference, Rosenblatt made rather strong statements that were reported by The New York Times as follows:

WASHINGTON, July 7 (UPI) – The Navy revealed the embryo of an electronic computer today that it expects will be able to walk, talk, see, write, reproduce itself and be conscious of its existence.

These comments caused scepticism among some researchers, including Minsky and Papert. In 1969, Minsky and Papert published the book *Perceptrons: An Introduction to computational geometry*. The book used mathematics, notably topology and group theory, to prove some results about the capabilities and limitations of simple networks of perceptrons.

It contained some positive, but also negative results:

- A single perceptron is incapable of implementing some predicates, such as the XOR logical function.
- Predicates such as parity and connectedness also cause serious difficulties for perceptrons.

The publication of the book led to the "XOR affair". In the words of Henning Dekant, the story that circulates goes like this: "Marvin Minsky, being a proponent of structured AI, killed off the connectionism approach [i.e., the one based on neural networks] when he co-authored the now classic tome, *Perceptrons*. This was accomplished by mathematically proving that a single layer perceptron is so limited it cannot even be used (or trained for that matter) to emulate an XOR gate. Although this does not hold for multi-layer perceptrons, his word was taken as gospel, and smothered this promising field in its infancy."

Marvin Minsky begs to differ, and argues that he of course knew about the capabilities of artificial neural networks with more than one layer, and that if anything, only the proof that working with local neurons comes at the cost of some universality should have any bearing.

Indeed, the earlier work of Warren McCulloch and Walter Pitts had already shown that neural networks were Turing-capable (i.e. constituted Turing machines).

Critics of the 1969 book posed other arguments that its publication, either intentionally or unintentionally, led to a decline in neural networks research for a decade. In his review of the book's 1988 expanded edition, Jordan B. Pollack, a proponent of connectionism, writes that

> Minsky and Papert surrounded their 1969 mathematical tract with fairly negative judgements and loaded terms, such as the following quotes, which have been used as evidence that they actually intended to stifle research on perceptron-like models.
>
> o Perceptrons have been widely publicized as "pattern recognition" or "learning" machines and as such have been discussed in a large number of books, journal articles, and voluminous "reports". Most of this writing... is without scientific value. (p. 4)

- We do not see that any good can come of experiments which pay no attention to limiting factors that will assert themselves as soon as the small model is scaled up to a usable size. (p. 18)
- [We] became involved with a somewhat therapeutic compulsion: to dispel what we feared to be the first shadows of a "holistic" or "Gestalt" misconception that would threaten to haunt the fields of engineering and artificial intelligence... (p. 20)
- There is no reason to suppose that any of these virtues carry over to the many layered version. Nevertheless, we consider it to be an important research problem to elucidate (or reject) our intuitive judgement that the extension is sterile. (p. 231)

Pollack continues:

> Despite these pronouncements, in 1988, Minsky and Papert wish to deny their responsibility, or, at least, their intentionality, in bringing about the decade-long connectionist winter:
>
> - One popular version is that the publication of our book so discouraged research on learning in network machines that a promising line of research was interrupted. Our version is that progress had already come to a virtual halt because of the lack of adequate basic theories.
>
> ...the real problem which terminated the research viability of perceptron-like models was the problem of scaling. Minsky and Papert asserted that as such learning models based on gradient descent in weight space were scaled up, they would be impractical due to local minimal extremely large weights and a concurrent growth in convergence time.
>
> So were they responsible for killing Snow White? No, since intention and action are separable, they were no more

responsible than Bill, who, intending to kill his uncle, is "so nervous and excited [when driving] that he accidentally runs over and kills a pedestrian, who happens to be his uncle". If Minsky and Papert did not intend to stifle the field of neural networks, then, perhaps, they would act in accordance with their new motto: "We see no reason to choose sides"

but agrees that "*Perceptrons*, and its authors, certainly have their places assured in history."

Whatever the reason, neural networks became unpopular in the 1970s, and few research groups continued research on this subject.

There were some exceptions. Stephen Grossberg developed a self-organizing neural network model known as Adaptive Resonance Theory (ART). Teuvo Kohonen worked on matrix-associative memories and self-organization of neurons into topological and tonotopical mappings of their perceived environment. However, much of the research attention focused elsewhere.

Chapter 9: The AI winters

In 1956, Herb Simon, one of the "fathers of artificial intelligence", predicted that within ten years computers would beat the world chess champion, compose "aesthetically satisfying" original music, and prove new mathematical theorems. It took forty years, not ten, but all these goals were achieved – and within a few years of each other! The music composed by David Cope's programs cannot be distinguished, even by professors of music, from that composed by Mozart, Beethoven, and Bach. In 1976, a computer was used in the proof of the long-unsolved "four colour problem."

Michael J. Beeson, *The Mechanization of Mathematics* in *Alan Turing: Life and Legacy of a Great Thinker* (2004)

The chapter delves into the history of machine translation during the Cold War, with the US government's keen interest in instantly translating Russian documents. Researchers initially optimistic about breakthroughs faced challenges in word-sense disambiguation, leading to translation errors. The National Research Council's Automatic Language Processing Advisory Committee (ALPAC) was formed in 1964 to assess the progress. Their 1966 report concluded that machine translation was costlier, less accurate, and slower than human translation. The chapter highlights the ALPAC report's impact, leading to the end of government support and the closure of AI research programs. The narrative then shifts to the Lighthill report of 1973, which critically evaluated AI research, emphasizing the disappointment in achieving promised breakthroughs and addressing the challenge of combinatorial explosion. The report significantly influenced the British government's decision to reduce support for AI research in universities.

During the Cold War, the US government was particularly interested in the automatic, instant translation of Russian documents and scientific reports. The government aggressively supported efforts at machine translation starting in 1954. At the outset, the researchers were optimistic. Noam Chomsky's new work in grammar was streamlining the translation process and there were many predictions of imminent breakthroughs.

However, researchers had underestimated the profound difficulty of word-sense disambiguation. In order to translate a sentence, a machine needed to have some idea what the sentence was about, otherwise it made mistakes. An apocryphal example is "the spirit is willing but the flesh is weak." Translated back and forth with Russian, it became "the vodka is good but the meat is rotten." Later researchers would call this the commonsense knowledge problem.

By 1964, the National Research Council had become concerned about the lack of progress and formed the Automatic Language Processing Advisory Committee (ALPAC) to look into the problem. They concluded, in a famous 1966 report, that machine translation was more expensive, less accurate, and slower than human translation. After spending some 20 million dollars, the NRC ended all support. Careers were destroyed and research ended.

> A recent study by the American Institutes for Research [D.B. Orr and V.H. Small, "A Reading Comprehension Test," Prelim. Rept., Contr. No. AF30 (602-3459), June 30 1965] had as its principal objective comparison of the accuracy and speed with which the same Russian documents can be read when they have been translated into English by the [USAF Foreign Technology Division (FTD)] machine translation (MT) system (one set postedited, the other set just as it came

out of the computer) and when they had been translated into English by a human translator in the conventional manner.

In physics, tests showed that the reader of raw MT output was 10 percent less accurate, 21 percent slower, and had a comprehension level 29 percent lower than when he used human translation. When he used postedited output, he was 3 percent less accurate, 11 percent slower, and had a comprehension level 13 percent lower than when he used human translation.

In the earth sciences, when he used raw MT output, he was 16 percent less accurate, 21 percent slower, and had a 25 percent lower comprehension level than when he used human translations. When he used postedited output, he was 5 percent less accurate, 11 percent slower, and had a comprehension level 23 percent lower than when he read human translations.

Subjectively a lot of the trouble seems to lie in unnatural constructions and unnatural word order, though strange translations of individual words or multiple translations of one word, with the choice left to the reader, are bothersome.

The *Lighthill report* is the name commonly used for the paper *Artificial Intelligence: A General Survey* by James Lighthill, published in *Artificial Intelligence: a paper symposium* in 1973.

Published in 1973, it was compiled by Lighthill for the British Science Research Council as an evaluation of the academic research in the field of artificial intelligence. The report gave a very pessimistic prognosis for many core aspects of research in this field, stating that "In no part of the field have the discoveries made so far produced the major impact that was then promised."

It "formed the basis for the decision by the British government to end support for AI research in most British universities." While the report was supportive of research into the simulation of neurophysiological and psychological processes, it was "highly critical of basic research in foundational areas such as robotics and language processing." The report stated that AI researchers had failed to address the issue of combinatorial explosion when

> Most workers in AI research and in related fields confess to a pronounced feeling of disappointment in what has been achieved in the past twenty-five years. Workers entered the field around 1950, and even around 1960, with high hopes that are very far from having realised in 1972. In no part of the field have the discoveries made so far produced the major impact that was then promised.

One particular "cause for disappointments" was singled out:

> failure to recognise the implications of the combinatorial explosion. This is a general obstacle to the construction of a self-organising system of a large knowledge base which results from the explosive growth of any combinatorial expression, representing numbers of possible ways of grouping elements of the knowledge base according to particular rules, as the base's size increases.

Chapter 10: Probability theory

> Archimedes will be remembered when Aeschylus is forgotten, because languages die and mathematical ideas do not. 'Immortality' may be a silly word, but probably a mathematician has the best chance of whatever it may mean.
>
> G.H. Hardy

The chapter explores the transition from logical reasoning to probability theory in the context of machine learning. It begins by illustrating logical arguments like modus ponens and modus tollens and then highlights their limitations in addressing uncertainties inherent in real-life situations. Probability theory, a branch of mathematics concerned with uncertainty, is introduced as a crucial framework. The concept of probability is discussed, with various interpretations, such as the frequentist view linking probability to relative frequency and the Bayesian perspective considering it a measure of belief. The chapter emphasizes Andrey Nikolaevich Kolmogorov's contribution to developing probability as a mathematical discipline, focusing on its behavior rather than its philosophical interpretation. The narrative then connects probability theory to modern machine learning, explaining its necessity in handling uncertain and stochastic quantities, distinguishing between uncertainty and stochasticity. The chapter concludes with Ian Hacking's acknowledgment of statisticians' impact on changing reasoning and experimental approaches, shaping our understanding of the world.

Consider our *modus ponens* and *modus tollens* examples:

If today is Tuesday, then John will go to work.
Today is Tuesday.
Therefore, John will go to work.

And

If the dog detects an intruder, the dog will bark.
The dog did not bark.
Therefore, no intruder was detected by the dog.

These logical arguments miss an important aspect of reality: namely, that life is an uncertain business.

In reality we may find that John will go to work on a Tuesday with probability of 95%. In 5% of the cases, he may be prevented by sickness or unforeseen circumstances. The dog will bark in 80% of the cases when there is an intruder. There may also be a nonzero probability of a false alarm: the dog may bark in 10% of the cases when there is no-one around.

We have transitioned from the language of logic to the language of *probability theory* – the branch of mathematics concerned with probability.

You may ask: but what is *probability*? This is a question for a philosopher as much as it is a question for a mathematician. There are several *interpretations of probability*. A *frequentist* will posit that the probability of an event is its relative frequency over time. A *Bayesian* will define probability as the "degree of belief" of the individual assessing the uncertainty of a particular situation.

The Soviet mathematician Andrey Nikolaevich Kolmogorov (1903-1987) sidestepped these philosophical arguments. He argued that

> The theory of probability as mathematical discipline can and should be developed from axioms in exactly the same way as Geometry and Algebra.

In other words, to a mathematician (rather than a philosopher), it doesn't matter what probability really *is*; what matters is how it *behaves*. This realization gave rise to modern (axiomatic) probability, which Kolmogorov outlined in his *Grundbegriffe der Wahrscheinlichkeitsrechnung* (1933).

Whereas early work on artificial intelligence relied mostly on logic, modern machine learning is built on probability theory. Ian Goodfellow (b. 1985 or 1986), Yoshua Bengio (b. 1964), and Aaron Courville in their book *Deep Learning* explain why this is the case:

> Many branches of computer science deal mostly with entities that are entirely deterministic and certain. A programmer can usually safely assume that a CPU will execute each machine instruction flawlessly. Errors in hardware do occur but are rare enough that most software applications do not need to be designed to account for them. Given that many computer scientists and software engineers work in a relatively clean and certain environment, it can be surprising that machine learning makes heavy use of probability theory.
>
> Machine learning must always deal with uncertain quantities and sometimes stochastic (nondeterministic) quantities. Uncertainty and stochasticity can arise from many sources. Researchers have made compelling arguments for quantifying uncertainty using probability since at least the 1980s.

Uncertainty and stochasticity are not to be confused. You are *uncertain* when you lack sufficient knowledge. Even if your knowledge is sufficient, the system in question may be inherently variable and fully or partially unpredictable – that's *stochasticity*.

Ian Hacking opined that

> The quiet statisticians have changed the world, not by discovering new facts or technical developments but by changing the ways we reason, experiment, and form our opinions about it.

Chapter 11: Deep learning

> I have always been convinced that the only way to get artificial intelligence to work is to do the computation in a way similar to the human brain. That is the goal I have been pursuing. We are making progress, though we still have lots to learn about how the brain actually works.
>
> Geoffrey Hinton

The chapter delves into the evolution of artificial intelligence (AI) and machine learning (ML), focusing on pivotal developments in deep learning over the past several decades. It begins with the introduction of backpropagation by Paul John Werbos in 1971, its rediscovery in 1985, and subsequent refinement by Rumelhart, Hinton, and Williams in 1986. The chapter explores the emergence of the Hopfield network and its impact on neural network research. The transition from AI to ML is discussed, emphasizing the cautious embrace of the term ML as a more acceptable alternative. Deep learning, characterized by employing deep neural networks, becomes a central theme, with backpropagation playing a crucial role in making large-scale, multi-layer networks feasible. Key milestones, such as AlexNet's success in 2012, the introduction of Recurrent Neural Networks (RNNs) and Gated Recurrent Units (GRUs), and the advent of Deep Belief Networks, highlight the expanding capabilities of deep learning. The chapter covers significant breakthroughs in the 2010s, including Google Brain's DistBelief, sequence-to-sequence models, Generative Adversarial Networks (GANs), and the transformative developments of BERT, GPT-2, and GPT-3 in 2018. The progression continues with the introduction of EfficientNet in 2019, the application of transformer architectures to computer vision with Vision Transformer (ViT) in 2021, Neural Architecture

Search methods, and the rise of Self-Supervised Learning in the 2020s. The chapter concludes by recognizing various models as a testament to the remarkable progress in deep learning, acknowledging the global contributions that shape this ongoing transformative journey.

In 1971, Paul John Webos marked a significant milestone in the realm of artificial intelligence (AI) with the development of a method for training multilayer neural networks through backpropagation of errors. This breakthrough, detailed in his 1974 PhD thesis at Harvard University titled "Beyond Regression: New Tools for Prediction and Analysis in Behavioural Sciences," later found its place in his book "The Roots of Backpropagation." This method extended the capabilities of feedforward neural networks, propelling them beyond the constraints of the MRI rule.

The backpropagation technique, however, experienced a period of dormancy until its rediscovery by D. B. Parker in 1985, as documented in a technical report at MIT. Simultaneously, Yann LeCun, during his 1985 PhD studies, proposed an alternative version of the backpropagation algorithm, initially published in French. It was not until 1986 that David Rumelhart, Geoffrey Hinton, and Ronald Williams refined and popularized backpropagation in their paper "Learning representations by back-propagation of errors."

This refinement marked a major turning point, rendering it feasible to train large, multi-layer neural networks with heightened precision and nonlinearity. Backpropagation not only made neural networks scalable but also paved the way for applications that were once inconceivable.

The early 1980s witnessed the invention of the associative neural network, known as the Hopfield network, by John Hopfield. Contrary to focusing on individual neurons, Hopfield centered his attention on the collective action of the network, modeling it as an energy minimization process. The discovery of backpropagation and the Hopfield network injected new life into neural network research, rekindling interest and sparking a resurgence.

As advancements in neural networks gained momentum, the field transformed into what is now commonly referred to as Machine Learning (ML). Researchers, cautious after the highs and lows of AI, embraced the term ML as a more modest and acceptable alternative. Nidhi Chappell from Intel described the relationship between AI and ML, emphasizing that AI represents the intelligence, while ML embodies the algorithms supporting it.

The term "deep learning" emerged, designating machine learning employing deep neural networks (DNN) with multiple hidden layers between the input and output layers. These networks could model complex nonlinear relationships. Backpropagation played a pivotal role in making deep learning with these networks feasible.

One of the early public successes in deep learning came in 2012 when Alex Krizhevsky, a student of Geoffrey Hinton, developed AlexNet. This artificial neural network won the ImageNet challenge, showcasing the potential of convolutional neural networks in correctly identifying hand-annotated images.

Sepp Hochreiter and Jürgen Schmidhuber's work in 2000 laid the foundation for Recurrent Neural Networks (RNNs) in sequence learning tasks. Gated Recurrent Units (GRUs) emerged in 2009, addressing some issues with traditional RNNs and improving performance in various sequential tasks. Geoffrey Hinton, Simon Osindero, and Yee-Whye The introduced Deep Belief Networks in 2006, playing a key role in popularizing deep learning by providing a framework for training deep architectures layer by layer.

Google Brain's DistBelief in 2012 laid the groundwork for scalable and efficient training of deep neural networks. In 2014, Ilya Sutskever, Oriol Vinyals, and Quoc V. Le introduced the sequence-to-sequence model architecture, influential in natural language processing tasks like machine translation. The same year, Ian Goodfellow, Yoshua Bengio, and Aaron Courville revolutionized the field with Generative Adversarial Networks (GANs), introducing a generative model framework.

In 2018, BERT (Bidirectional Encoder Representations from Transformers) significantly improved natural language understanding, while GPT-2 and GPT-3, developed by the OpenAI Team in the same year, showcased the power of large-scale pre-trained language models.

EfficientNet (2019) by Mingxing Tan and Quoc V. Le introduced a scalable and efficient neural network architecture, balancing model size and performance. The application of transformer architectures to computer vision tasks, exemplified by the Vision Transformer (ViT) in 2021, challenged the dominance of convolutional neural networks.

The field of deep learning also saw the development of Neural Architecture Search methods in 2018, automating the process of designing neural network architectures. Self-Supervised Learning in the 2020s gained prominence for leveraging unannotated data, and T5 (Text-To-Text Transfer Transformer, 2019) introduced a unified approach to various language tasks.

BERT, GPT, EfficientNet, ViT, and various other models represent a snapshot of the remarkable progress in deep learning over the past two decades. Researchers and teams worldwide have contributed to shaping this transformative journey, and the story of deep learning continues to unfold with each passing breakthrough.

Chapter 12: Transformers and generative AI

> AI systems will become more intelligent than humans, but they will still be subservient to us.
>
> Yann LeCun on LinkedIn, 2023

The chapter explores the transformative impact of Transformers in the realm of artificial intelligence (AI), particularly in the context of generative AI. Transformers, described as ingenious language artists and pattern recognizers, revolutionize how machines comprehend and generate information. Central to their prowess is the attention mechanism, functioning as a cognitive spotlight, allowing models to selectively focus on different facets of input data. This enables Transformers to excel in language tasks, such as translation and content creation, by capturing intricate patterns and contextual relationships. Generative AI, fueled by Transformers, ventures into diverse domains, from language translation to image synthesis, artistic creations, music composition, and even drug discovery. The chapter acknowledges the remarkable achievements of generative AI models, including OpenAI's GPT-3 and projects like DALL-E and StyleGAN, showcasing their versatility and creativity. While celebrating these milestones, the chapter emphasizes the ethical considerations and limitations of these technologies, paving the way for continuous evolution and exciting possibilities in the dynamic field of generative AI.

In the dynamic landscape of artificial intelligence, Transformers stand out as remarkable models that have revolutionized the way computers comprehend and generate information. These sophisticated systems can be likened to ingenious language artists and pattern recognizers, empowering machines to navigate complex relationships within data and produce imaginative outputs.

Consider the task of teaching a computer to understand language or create art. Traditionally, machines grappled with the complexity of long sentences or intricate patterns. Then emerged the Transformers, inspired by human information processing, excelling at capturing the contextual nuances of words and the intricate connections between them.

At the heart of what makes Transformers special lies their attention mechanism – a virtual spotlight that allows the model to focus on different facets of input when making predictions or generating content. This attention to detail enables Transformers to comprehend the meaning of words in context, transforming them into exceptional storytellers or adept translators.

Now, let's delve into the realm of generative AI, often considered the AI's imagination – the capability to craft something entirely new, whether it be a piece of writing, an image, or even music. Fuelled by models like Transformers, generative AI possesses the ability to draw inspiration from existing data and conjure entirely novel, often surprisingly creative content.

Imagine presenting the AI with a sentence or a prompt, and rather than regurgitating information, it generates something entirely fresh based on its learning. It's akin to having a machine that can compose unique stories, paint imaginary landscapes, or even dream up new inventions.

The strides made in generative AI, propelled by Transformers, find applications in diverse domains such as language translation, content creation, and beyond. These models, akin to the artistic side of AI, empower machines not only to comprehend but also to create. This opens up exciting possibilities for innovation and collaboration between humans and machines, ushering in a new era of creativity.

Underlying the transformative capabilities of Transformers is their attention mechanism. This mechanism acts as a cognitive spotlight, enabling the model to selectively focus on different parts of input data, a crucial feature for capturing intricate patterns and contextual relationships.

Let's consider specific instances where generative AI, driven by Transformers, has made a substantial impact. In the field of language translation, these models excel at providing nuanced and context-aware translations, overcoming challenges that traditional methods faced with idiomatic expressions and cultural nuances. In content creation, imagine an AI-driven system crafting compelling narratives or generating visually stunning artwork, all inspired by its learned patterns and creativity.

While Transformers have showcased remarkable capabilities, it's essential to acknowledge that, like any technology, they have limitations. There may be scenarios where these models struggle, and ethical considerations surrounding their applications warrant careful attention.

The journey doesn't end here. The field of generative AI, propelled by Transformers, is on a trajectory of continuous evolution. Anticipating future developments and trends promises even more exciting possibilities, underscoring the dynamic nature of this innovative technology.

To aid in grasping these concepts, consider visualizing the attention mechanism through simple diagrams or illustrations. These visuals can provide a tangible representation of how Transformers selectively attend to different elements in input data.

Transformers in AI are not just models; they are engines of creativity and understanding. By addressing technical nuances, providing concrete examples, acknowledging limitations, looking ahead to the future, and incorporating visuals, this exploration aims to paint a more comprehensive picture of the transformative impact and potential of Transformers in the realm of generative AI.

Generative AI has achieved remarkable milestones, showcasing its versatility and creativity.

Generative AI models, particularly those based on transformer architectures, have excelled in language translation tasks. They can translate text between multiple languages with impressive accuracy, capturing nuances and context.

Models like OpenAI's GPT-3 have demonstrated the ability to generate coherent and contextually relevant text. From creative writing to news articles, these models can produce human-like language based on prompts.

Generative Adversarial Networks (GANs) have been instrumental in generating realistic images. StyleGAN, for instance, can create high-quality, diverse images, showcasing advancements in image synthesis.

AI has ventured into the realm of art, generating paintings, drawings, and other artistic creations. Projects like DALL-E, also by OpenAI, can generate images based on textual descriptions, demonstrating creativity in the visual arts.

Generative AI has made strides in composing music. AI systems can analyze musical patterns and generate original compositions, blurring the lines between machine-generated and human-created music.

From writing code snippets to generating marketing content, generative AI models have found applications across diverse domains. They can assist with content creation, making them valuable tools in professional settings.

AI has been employed to assist in the design of video game elements, including characters, levels, and scenarios. This not only speeds up the game development process but also introduces novel and unexpected elements.

Generative AI has shown promise in drug discovery by predicting molecular structures and potential drug candidates. This application accelerates the identification of new compounds for pharmaceutical purposes.

While controversial, deepfake technology powered by generative AI has demonstrated the ability to manipulate video content, placing faces onto different bodies or altering expressions. This has implications for both entertainment and potential misuse.

Generative AI models contribute to natural language understanding, enabling more sophisticated human-computer interactions. Virtual assistants and chatbots leverage these capabilities to provide more context-aware and nuanced responses.

These achievements illustrate the diverse and impactful capabilities of generative AI across various domains, shaping the landscape of technology and creativity.

Chapter 13: ChatGPT and other LLMs

> ChatGPT is scary good. We are not far from dangerously strong AI.
>
> Elon Musk

> ChatGPT is incredibly limited, but good enough at some things to create a misleading impression of greatness. It's a mistake to be relying on it for anything important right now. It's a preview of progress; we have lots of work to do on robustness and truthfulness.
>
> Sam Altman, CEO of OpenAI, Twitter, 2022.10.12

The chapter introduces Large Language Models (LLMs) as revolutionary digital language wizards, highlighting their human-like understanding and creativity in processing language. Tracing the history of LLMs, it explores their evolution from statistical models to the transformative impact of neural networks and large-scale transformers. The narrative emphasizes key milestones, adaptability, and ethical considerations, anticipating ongoing advancements. The chapter also delves into the intriguing connection between language and decision-making, drawing insights from experiments challenging traditional notions of free will. Lastly, it discusses the role of LLMs and reinforcement learning in decision-making, noting their distinct strengths based on task requirements.

Large Language Models, or LLMs, are like digital language wizards, bringing an extraordinary level of understanding and creativity to computers when it comes to processing human language. These models represent a breakthrough in the field of artificial intelligence, designed to comprehend, generate, and interact with language in a way that seems surprisingly human-like.

Imagine having a conversation with a computer that not only understands what you say but can also respond in a coherent and contextually relevant manner. That's the magic of LLMs. They're like virtual language companions, capable of understanding the nuances, emotions, and intricacies of our words.

LLMs learn by reading and analyzing enormous amounts of text from the internet and other sources. This vast knowledge allows them to understand the richness and diversity of human language.

These models are masters of context. They don't just recognize individual words; they understand how words relate to each other in sentences and paragraphs, capturing the context and meaning behind the language.

LLMs aren't one-trick ponies. They can be adapted for various language-related tasks, such as answering questions, translating languages, summarizing text, or even engaging in casual conversation. Their versatility stems from a fundamental understanding of language.

One of the most fascinating aspects is their ability to generate new content. You can give them a prompt or ask them to continue a story, and they'll craft responses that feel surprisingly creative, as if they have a touch of artistic flair.

LLMs aim for a more natural and human-like interaction. They don't just provide robotic responses; instead, they generate text that feels more conversational, making interactions with computers feel more intuitive and engaging.

These language wizards are not just for entertainment. They can be powerful assistants in various fields, helping with tasks like drafting emails, writing code, or summarizing lengthy articles. They're like collaborative partners that enhance our capabilities.

As with any powerful tool, there are ethical considerations. Ensuring that LLMs are used responsibly and do not perpetuate biases present in their training data is an ongoing challenge. Researchers are actively working on making these models fair and unbiased.

In essence, LLMs are transforming the way computers understand and interact with language, bringing us closer to a future where seamless communication between humans and machines becomes a reality. They are at the forefront of AI, opening up exciting possibilities for innovation, creativity, and improved human-computer collaboration.

Language Models have evolved significantly over the years, and Large Language Models (LLMs) represent a recent and transformative development in the field of artificial intelligence. Let's take a journey through the history of LLMs.

In the early 2000s, statistical language models were prevalent, relying on mathematical probabilities to predict the next word in a sequence. These models had limitations in capturing complex linguistic nuances.

The breakthrough came with the resurgence of neural networks, particularly deep learning. Around 2010, researchers started using neural networks to model language, allowing machines to learn intricate patterns and representations of words.

Word embeddings, such as Word2Vec and GloVe, gained popularity. These techniques represented words as vectors in a high-dimensional space, capturing semantic relationships between words.

Researchers experimented with Recurrent Neural Networks (RNNs) in the mid-2010s. RNNs were designed to handle sequential data, making them suitable for language modeling. However, they faced challenges in capturing long-term dependencies.

In 2017, the introduction of the Transformer architecture by Vaswani et al. marked a significant turning point. Transformers, with their attention mechanism, overcame the limitations of RNNs, allowing models to consider the context of words more effectively.

Around the same time, pre-training and transfer learning became popular. Models were pre-trained on massive amounts of data in an unsupervised manner, learning a general understanding of language. This knowledge could then be fine-tuned for specific tasks.

In 2018, BERT (Bidirectional Encoder Representations from Transformers) emerged as a game-changer. Developed by Google, BERT focused on bidirectional learning, considering both the left and right context of words. This approach significantly improved language understanding and performance across various NLP tasks.

In 2020, OpenAI released GPT-3 (Generative Pre-trained Transformer 3), one of the largest LLMs to date, with a staggering 175 billion parameters. GPT-3 showcased the power of large-scale pre-training, generating coherent and contextually relevant text across diverse prompts.

LLMs started being fine-tuned for specific applications, including language translation, summarization, question-answering, and more. This adaptability showcased the versatility of LLMs across a wide range of language-related tasks.

As LLMs gained prominence, ethical concerns around bias, fairness, and responsible use emerged. Researchers and organizations began actively addressing these issues to ensure that LLMs are used ethically and avoid perpetuating biases present in training data.

The field of LLMs continues to evolve rapidly. Researchers are exploring new architectures, addressing ethical challenges, and working towards models that can understand and generate language in even more sophisticated ways.

In conclusion, the history of LLMs is a journey of innovation, from early statistical models to the transformative power of neural networks and large-scale transformers. These models have brought us closer to achieving natural and context-aware language understanding, opening up new frontiers in human-computer interaction and communication.

Transformers play a crucial role in large language models (LLMs) like ChatGPT.

Transformers serve as the foundational architecture for LLMs. The transformer architecture, introduced by Vaswani et al. in 2017, has become the go-to structure for natural language processing tasks.

The heart of transformers is the attention mechanism, allowing the model to focus on different parts of the input sequence when making predictions. This attention mechanism enables the model to capture long-range dependencies and understand the context of words in a more sophisticated way compared to previous architectures.

Transformers excel at capturing contextual information. Each word in a sequence is not processed in isolation; rather, its representation is influenced by the surrounding words. This contextual understanding is crucial for language models to generate coherent and contextually relevant responses.

Transformers address the challenge of long-term dependencies in sequences. Traditional recurrent neural networks (RNNs) struggle with maintaining information over long distances, but transformers handle this more effectively, making them suitable for tasks requiring understanding of broader context.

LLMs like ChatGPT use a two-step process: pre-training and fine-tuning. In the pre-training phase, the transformer model learns from massive amounts of text data, developing a general understanding of language. Fine-tuning is then performed on specific tasks or datasets to adapt the model for more specialized purposes.

Transformers enable efficient transfer learning. The pre-trained model, having learned from diverse data sources, can be fine-tuned for specific applications. This transfer learning approach allows models like ChatGPT to leverage knowledge gained from general language understanding tasks when generating responses in a conversational context.

Transformers are highly adaptable and can be used for various natural language processing tasks. Beyond conversational AI, they are employed in tasks such as translation, summarization, question-answering, and more. The same transformer architecture can be fine-tuned for different applications, showcasing its versatility.

The attention mechanism and contextual understanding of transformers contribute to the generation of coherent and contextually relevant text. In models like ChatGPT, transformers generate responses by considering the input context, making the conversation flow more naturally.

Transformers help LLMs handle ambiguity and ambivalence in language. The attention mechanism allows the model to weigh the importance of different words and phrases, enabling it to navigate and respond effectively to nuanced inputs.

In summary, transformers serve as the backbone for large language models like ChatGPT, providing the architecture and mechanisms necessary for understanding, generating, and adapting language in diverse and contextually rich ways.

While LLMs have gained such popularity as to dominate the present AI landscape (in 2024), the role of language in human decision-making remains somewhat controversial. One of the experiments that shed light on the idea that language might be a post-factum rationalization while decisions are made using a different mechanism in the brain is the study conducted by Benjamin Libet in the 1980s.

In Libet's experiments, participants were asked to perform a simple motor task, such as pressing a button, while the electrical activity in their brains was monitored using electroencephalography (EEG). What made these experiments particularly intriguing was the inclusion of a subjective timing element. Participants were also asked to report the moment when they consciously decided to perform the action.

The key finding of Libet's experiments was the observation of a readiness potential (RP), a gradual build-up of brain activity that occurred before the participants reported making a conscious decision to act. The RP suggested that the brain initiated the action before the participant was aware of the decision.

Furthermore, the reported time of conscious awareness of the decision lagged behind the onset of the RP. This temporal discrepancy led to the conclusion that the brain had already initiated the motor action before the conscious decision was formed. In other words, the conscious awareness of the decision appeared to be a post-factum event, raising questions about the true nature of the decision-making process and the role of conscious experience in initiating actions.

These findings challenged traditional notions of free will and conscious decision-making, suggesting that the brain might engage in preconscious processes that lead to actions, with the conscious mind later rationalizing and attributing these actions. It sparked debates and discussions about the intricate relationship between consciousness, decision-making, and the brain's neural processes.

What makes Libet's work particularly relevant to the role of language in decision-making is a subsequent experiment conducted by Chun Siong Soon and colleagues in 2008. They used a similar setup but introduced a twist: participants were asked to report the moment they became aware of their decision to move. Surprisingly, the researchers found that the readiness potential still preceded the conscious awareness of the decision, but there was also brain activity in the prefrontal cortex that occurred just before the reported moment of decision.

This experiment indicated that the prefrontal cortex, a region associated with higher cognitive functions, was involved in the process of becoming consciously aware of a decision. While there is ongoing debate about the interpretation of these findings and their implications for free will, Libet's work and subsequent studies have contributed valuable insights into the neural mechanisms underlying decision-making and the subsequent verbalization of those decisions.

At the time of writing, there isn't a clear and universally accepted argument asserting the provable optimality of Large Language Models (LLMs) versus reinforcement learning (RL) for decision-making across all contexts. Both LLMs and RL serve distinct purposes, and their optimal use depends on the nature of the task and the available data.

LLMs, such as GPT-3, are proficient in natural language understanding and generation. They excel in tasks related to language processing, content creation, and information retrieval. Their pre-trained knowledge allows them to generate coherent and contextually relevant responses. However, their application to decision-making may lack the structured and goal-oriented nature often required in certain domains.

Reinforcement learning, on the other hand, is a powerful paradigm for training agents to make decisions through trial and error. RL is well-suited for tasks where an agent must learn from interactions with an environment to maximize a cumulative reward. It is frequently employed in areas like robotics, game playing, and autonomous systems.

The optimal choice between LLMs and RL for decision-making hinges on the specific requirements of the task. LLMs might be preferable when the decision-making process involves understanding and generating natural language, while RL might be more suitable for scenarios requiring sequential decision-making and learning from interactions.

Chapter 14: Reinforcement Learning

...in 1979 we came to realize that perhaps the simplest of the ideas, which had long been taken for granted, had received surprisingly little attention from a computational perspective. This was simply the idea of a learning system that *wants* something, that adapts its behavior in order to maximize a special signal from its environment. This was the idea of a "hedonistic" learning system, or, as we would say now, the idea of reinforcement learning.

Richard S. Sutton and Andrew G. Barto, *Reinforcement Learning: An Introduction*

The chapter explores the concept of Reinforcement Learning (RL), likening it to training a pet through rewards for good choices. It emphasizes RL's role in enabling computers to learn and improve by interacting with environments, drawing parallels with teaching a dog tricks. The goal-oriented nature of RL, where a computer aims to accomplish specific tasks through trial and error, is highlighted. The chapter explains the balance between exploration and exploitation in RL, akin to a journey of discovering the best paths. RL's applications beyond games, including self-driving cars, robotics, and optimizing complex systems, are discussed. It concludes by portraying RL as a challenging yet rewarding endeavor in the field of artificial intelligence. Additionally, the chapter explores the historical influence of Alan Turing's theoretical contributions on the development of RL, emphasizing the alignment of Turing's ideas with the broader goals of machine intelligence and decision-making. The evolution of RL over decades, marked by key milestones, is outlined, showcasing its diverse applications, from game playing to complex real-world scenarios. The pivotal role of Richard S. Sutton and Andrew G. Barto in shaping RL, notably their contributions to Temporal Difference learning, Actor-Critic architectures, exploration strategies, eligibility traces, N-step methods, and policy gradient methods, is highlighted. The chapter concludes by underlining Sutton and Barto's lasting impact on the reinforcement learning community, not only through their research but also through mentorship, teaching, and engagement with the broader research community.

Reinforcement Learning is like teaching a computer to make decisions by rewarding it for good choices, much like training a pet. It's a powerful concept in artificial intelligence that allows machines to learn and improve through experience, just like we do.

Imagine you're training a dog to perform tricks. When the dog does something you like, you give it a treat. Over time, the dog learns to associate good behaviour with rewards. Reinforcement learning works somewhat similarly but with computers and algorithms.

In reinforcement learning, a computer, or an agent, interacts with an environment. It tries different actions and learns from the outcomes, whether good or bad. It's like the computer is playing a game, trying to figure out the best moves to win.

Just like with the dog and the treats, the computer gets rewards when it makes good decisions and achieves its goals. These rewards encourage the computer to repeat those actions in the future. On the flip side, if it makes a mistake, it might receive a "punishment" in the form of a negative score, encouraging it to avoid those actions.

Reinforcement learning is goal-oriented. The computer has a specific objective or task, and its goal is to figure out the best way to accomplish it. This could be anything from playing a game, driving a car, or even managing resources efficiently.

To learn effectively, the computer needs to balance exploration and exploitation. It tries new things to discover what works well, but it also sticks to actions that have proven to be successful. It's like trying different paths on a journey, learning which ones lead to the best destinations.

The computer, through reinforcement learning, becomes like a decision-making expert. It learns over time to make better choices by understanding the consequences of its actions and adjusting its strategies based on what leads to positive outcomes.

Reinforcement learning isn't just for games. It's used in self-driving cars to learn how to navigate traffic, in robotics for tasks like grasping objects, and even in optimizing complex systems like energy grids or financial portfolios.

Just like us, computers face challenges in learning. They might make mistakes along the way, but that's part of the learning process. Reinforcement learning is like a challenging puzzle for computers, making it both a serious and fun endeavour in the world of artificial intelligence.

Reinforcement learning is a fascinating approach that enables computers to learn by doing, receiving rewards for good choices, and gradually becoming adept decision-makers. It's a key ingredient in creating intelligent systems that can tackle complex tasks and improve their performance over time.

Alan Turing, a pioneering figure in computer science and artificial intelligence, laid the foundational principles for computation and machine intelligence. While he did not directly contribute to the development of reinforcement learning as we understand it today, his work and ideas have had a profound influence on the broader field of artificial intelligence, setting the stage for subsequent advancements, including reinforcement learning. Here's an outline of how Alan Turing's contributions have influenced the development of reinforcement learning.

Turing's groundbreaking concept of a universal machine, articulated in his famous 1936 paper "On Computable Numbers," laid the theoretical groundwork for modern computers. His idea of a machine capable of executing any algorithm provided the theoretical basis for the computational systems that later became essential for implementing reinforcement learning algorithms.

Turing introduced the concept of the Turing Test in his 1950 paper "Computing Machinery and Intelligence." While the Turing Test is more closely associated with natural language processing and general AI, the pursuit of machine intelligence and the ability to make decisions aligns with the broader goals of reinforcement learning.

Turing Machines, a theoretical construct introduced by Turing, helped establish the theoretical limits and possibilities of computation. Understanding the fundamentals of computation is crucial for developing algorithms, including those used in reinforcement learning, where efficient computation is essential for decision-making.

Turing's work emphasized the importance of formalizing algorithms and processes. This emphasis on algorithmic thinking and formal methods has played a pivotal role in shaping the approach to developing reinforcement learning algorithms, which rely on well-defined processes for learning and decision-making.

Turing's contributions to the theoretical foundations of computation provided a solid base for the development of machine learning algorithms. Reinforcement learning, as a subset of machine learning, leverages these theoretical foundations to design algorithms that enable systems to learn and make decisions in dynamic environments.

Turing's exploration of universal learning machines in his 1936 paper foreshadows the concept of agents in reinforcement learning that can learn and adapt to different environments. While not directly influencing specific reinforcement learning algorithms, his ideas contributed to the broader understanding of machine learning.

While Alan Turing did not directly contribute to the development of reinforcement learning as a specific field, his groundbreaking work in computation, algorithms, and machine intelligence has profoundly influenced the broader landscape of artificial intelligence. The principles and theoretical foundations laid by Turing continue to guide researchers and practitioners in the design and implementation of intelligent systems, including those involved in reinforcement learning.

Reinforcement Learning (RL) has a rich history that spans several decades, marked by key milestones and influential contributions.

The roots of reinforcement learning can be traced back to the 1950s and 1960s. Early work by researchers such as Richard Bellman laid the foundation for dynamic programming, a mathematical framework used to solve problems involving sequential decision-making. Bellman's work provided the groundwork for formalizing the RL problem.

The concept of Temporal Difference (TD) learning was introduced by Richard Sutton in the early 1980s. TD learning became a pivotal element in RL algorithms, allowing agents to learn from experiences over time and update their estimates of expected rewards. This work contributed to the development of model-free reinforcement learning.

In 1989, Christopher Watkins introduced Q-learning, an influential model-free RL algorithm. Q-learning aimed to find the optimal action-selection policy for a given finite Markov decision process. Q-learning became a fundamental algorithm and laid the groundwork for subsequent developments in RL.

In the 1990s, researchers explored evolutionary strategies and neuroevolution as approaches to reinforcement learning.

Evolutionary methods, inspired by natural selection, sought to evolve policies and strategies for decision-making. Neuroevolution involved evolving neural network structures and parameters to enhance learning.

Reinforcement learning gained attention for its application in game playing during this period. Gerald Tesauro's work on TD-Gammon demonstrated the ability of RL to achieve superhuman performance in backgammon. This success showcased the potential of RL in complex decision-making tasks.

Deep Q Networks, introduced by Volodymyr Mnih and others at DeepMind in 2013, marked a significant breakthrough. DQN combined Q-learning with deep neural networks, enabling RL in environments with high-dimensional state spaces. This work demonstrated successful RL applications, particularly in playing Atari 2600 games.

DeepMind's AlphaGo, the RL-powered system that defeated a world champion Go player in 2016, was a watershed moment. The success of AlphaGo highlighted the power of RL in mastering complex strategic games and showcased its potential in real-world applications.

PPO and TRPO, introduced in 2017, are advanced policy optimization algorithms that gained popularity for their stability and efficiency in training deep RL models. These algorithms addressed challenges associated with policy gradient methods and contributed to the success of RL in various domains.

OpenAI's contributions to reinforcement learning, including the development of models like Proximal Policy Optimization (PPO) and the exploration of RL in complex environments like robotics, have been influential. Models like OpenAI Five showcased RL's potential in collaborative decision-making.

The 2020s continue to witness ongoing advances in deep reinforcement learning. Researchers are exploring more sophisticated algorithms, addressing challenges such as sample efficiency, generalization, and safe exploration. RL applications span diverse domains, including robotics, healthcare, finance, and more.

The history of reinforcement learning is characterized by a progression from early theoretical foundations to the development of practical algorithms and their successful applications in complex real-world scenarios. The continuous evolution of RL reflects its significance in shaping the landscape of artificial intelligence and autonomous decision-making.

Sutton and Barto co-authored the textbook "Reinforcement Learning: An Introduction," first published in 1998 and later revised in 2018. This comprehensive and widely-used textbook provides an in-depth and accessible exploration of the fundamental concepts, algorithms, and applications of reinforcement learning. It has become a foundational resource for students, researchers, and practitioners in the field.

In the late 1980s, Richard S. Sutton introduced Temporal Difference (TD) learning, a crucial concept in reinforcement learning. TD learning is a model-free approach that allows agents to learn directly from experiences, estimating the value function by updating predictions based on the difference between current and predicted future rewards. This work laid the groundwork for subsequent advancements in RL.

Sutton has contributed significantly to the development and popularization of Actor-Critic architectures in reinforcement learning. Actor-Critic models combine value-based methods (Critic) with policy-based methods (Actor), providing a more versatile and stable approach to learning in complex environments.

Both Sutton and Barto have made contributions to the understanding of exploration strategies in reinforcement learning. They explored the delicate balance between exploration and exploitation, crucial for agents to discover optimal policies in unknown environments.

Sutton's work on eligibility traces, a mechanism for efficiently updating value estimates in TD learning, has been influential. Eligibility traces help address the credit assignment problem, allowing the algorithm to attribute rewards to relevant actions more effectively.

Sutton has also contributed to the development of N-step methods in reinforcement learning. N-step methods generalize TD learning by incorporating information from multiple consecutive time steps, providing a trade-off between bias and variance in value estimation.

Barto has conducted research on policy gradient methods, focusing on algorithms that directly optimize policies in reinforcement learning. Policy gradient methods, a subset of reinforcement learning, aim to find policies that maximize the expected cumulative reward.

Sutton and Barto have played a crucial role in the reinforcement learning community. They have contributed not only through their research but also through mentorship, teaching, and engagement with the broader research community. Their influence extends to their association with OpenAI, contributing to the organization's mission of advancing artificial intelligence in a safe and beneficial manner.

Chapter 15: GPUs

Your free lunch will soon be over. What can you do about it? What *are* you doing about it? The major processor manufacturers and architectures, from Intel and AMD to Sparc and PowerPC, have run out of room with most of their traditional approaches to boosting CPU performance. Instead of driving clock speeds and straight-line instruction throughput ever higher, they are instead turning *en masse* to hyperthreading and multicore architectures.

Herb Sutter

The chapter delves into the evolution and architecture of central processing units (CPUs) in computers. Highlighting the consistent role of CPUs as the brains of modern computers, the chapter outlines the key components, including the arithmetic and logical unit (ALU), processor registers, and the control unit (CU). It explains the hierarchical structure of memory, featuring processor registers, caches, and main memory, emphasizing the trade-offs between speed and capacity. The significance of clock rates in measuring processor speed is discussed, spanning from hertz in early computers to gigahertz in the 21st century. The chapter explores the transition to multicore processors, focusing on increased core count rather than clock rates. It extends the concept to graphics processing units (GPUs), initially developed for graphics manipulation but evolving into powerful parallel processors. The emergence of general-purpose computing on GPUs (GPGPU) is explored, including Nvidia's CUDA platform and applications like cryptocurrency mining and deep learning.

The chapter concludes by introducing new-age devices such as Field Programmable Gate Arrays (FPGAs), Application Specific Integrated Circuits (ASICs), Tensor Processing Units (TPUs), and Intelligence Processing Units (IPUs), with a glimpse into Quantum Processing Units (QPUs) and quantum machine learning.

In the chapter on computers we have seen many distinct computing devices. Yet they have something in common: they all have some form of a CPU. The *central processing unit (CPU)* is the brain of a modern computer. Its job is to execute instructions comprising a computer program. The CPU performs basic arithmetic, logic, controlling, and input/output (I/O) operations specified by the instructions in the program.

The form, design, and implementation of CPUs have changed over time, but their fundamental operation remains almost unchanged. Principal components of a CPU include the *arithmetic and logical unit (ALU)* that performs arithmetic and logic operations, processor *registers* that supply operands to the ALU and store the results of ALU operations, and a *control unit (CU)* that orchestrates the fetching (from memory) and execution of instructions by directing the coordinated operations of the ALU, registers, and other components.

Processor registers are quickly accessible locations available to the CPU. They are placed inside the processor. Processor registers are at the top of the *memory hierarchy*, and provide the fastest way to access data. *Main memory* is external to the CPU. Modern processors use either static or dynamic random-access memory (RAM) as main memory, with the latter usually accessed via one or more cache levels.

Processor cache is an intermediate stage between the ultra-fast registers and much slower main memory. It was introduced to improve the performance of computers. Most actively used information in the main memory is duplicated in the cache memory, which is faster, but of much lesser capacity. On the other hand, main memory is much slower, but has a much greater storage capacity than processor registers. Multi-level hierarchical cache setup is commonly used – *primary cache* being smallest, fastest, and located inside the processor; *secondary cache* being somewhat larger and slower.

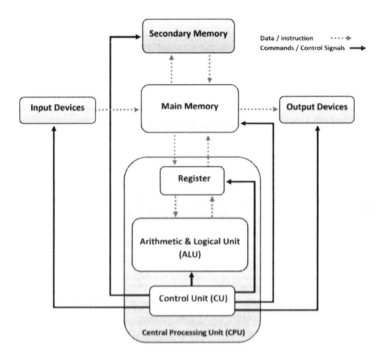

In computation, time is of the essence. The *clock rate* refers to the frequency at which the clock generator of a processor can generate pulses, which are used to synchronize the operations of its components, and is used as an indicator of the processor's speed. It is measured in *clock cycles per second* or its equivalent, the SI unit hertz (Hz).

The clock rate of the first generation of computers was measured in hertz or kilohertz (kHz), the first personal computers (PCs) to arrive throughout the 1970s and 1980s had clock rates measured in megahertz (MHz), and in the 21st century the speed of modern CPUs is commonly advertised in gigahertz (GHz).

In 2001, IBM introduced the world's first multicore processor, a chip with two 64-bit microprocessors comprising more than 170 million transistors. A *multicore* processor is a computer processor on a single integrated circuit with two or more separate processing units (called *cores*), each of which reads and executes program instructions. The instructions are ordinary CPU instructions but the single processor can run instructions on separate cores at the same time, increasing overall speed for programs that support *parallel computing* – a type of computation in which many calculations are carried out simultaneously.

Since 2001, the focus has been less on increasing the clock rates, more on increasing the number of cores. Most modern processors are multicore, including those found in modern devices. It is not uncommon nowadays to have a *multiprocessor* system with multiple multicore processors:

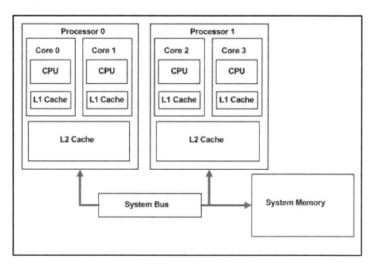

The multicore idea has been taken to the extreme in *graphics processing units (GPUs)*. In the 1970s, the term GPU described a programmable processing unit working independently from the CPU and responsible for graphics manipulation and output. Many graphics operations are easily parallelizable, so GPUs have evolved to operated at lower frequencies than CPUs, but they typically have many times the number of cores. GPUs can process far more pictures and graphical data per second than a traditional CPU.

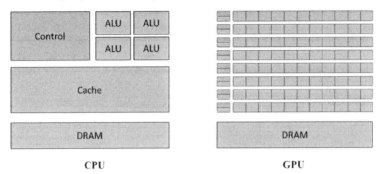

CPU   GPU

The evolution of GPUs was initially driven by the gaming industry. The 1990s saw the *3D revolution* where 3D polygon graphics became the *de facto* standard for video game visual presentation. The first-person shooter genre takes its origin from Wolfenstein 3D (1992), which created the genre's basic archetype upon which subsequent titles were based.

General-purpose computing on graphics processing units (GPGPU) is the use of a GPU to perform computation in non-graphics applications traditionally handled by the central processing unit (CPU). The use of multiple video cards in one computer, or large numbers of graphics chips, further parallelizes the already parallel nature of graphics processing.

In 2007 Nvidia released *CUDA (Compute Unified Device Architecture)*, a parallel computing platform that allows software developers to use a CUDA-enabled graphics processing unit (GPU) for general purpose processing. Most modern Nvidia GPUs are CUDA-capable.

Cryptocurrency mining was originally performed using CPUs. However, their limited processing speed and high power consumption led to limited output, rendering the CPU-based mining process inefficient. A standard GPU, like a Radeon HD 5970, clocked processing speeds of executing 3,200 32-bit instructions per clock, which was 800 times more than the speed of a CPU that executed only 4 32-bit instructions per clock. It is this property of the GPUs that makes them suitable and better for cryptocurrency mining, as the mining process requires higher efficiency in performing similar kinds of repetitive computations. The mining device continuously tries to decode different hashes repeatedly with only one digit changing in each attempt.

A BitFarm in Canada

Deep learning is another major user of GPGPU. GPU-accelerated deep learning frameworks offer flexibility to design and train custom deep neural networks and provide interfaces to commonly-used programming languages such as Python and C/C++. Every major deep learning framework such as TensorFlow, PyTorch, and others, are already GPU-accelerated, so data scientists and researchers can be productive in minutes without any GPU programming.

GPUs have been around for years, but face competition from improved, new-age devices. They include the Field Programmable Gate Arrays (FPGAs), Application Specific Integrated Circuits (ASICs), Google's Tensor Processing Units (TPUs), and Graphcore's Intelligence Processing Units (IPUs). Nowadays people are beginning to talk about Quantum Processing Units (QPU) and quantum machine learning.

Chapter 16: Real-time AI, FPGAs and ASICs

> Business at the speed of thought is a digital nervous system – a real-time and complete information flow.
>
> Bill Gates, *Business at the Speed of Thought*

The chapter explores the concept of real-time AI, emphasizing its critical role in applications requiring instantaneous processing and decision-making. Real-time AI systems operate with minimal latency, making quick decisions in the order of milliseconds to microseconds. The significance of low latency is highlighted in diverse fields such as autonomous vehicles, financial trading, healthcare monitoring, and industrial automation. The chapter contrasts real-time AI with batch processing, underlining the continuous analysis of incoming data and the ability to dynamically adapt to changing conditions. Various applications of real-time AI, including speech and image recognition, fraud detection, video surveillance, and gaming, are discussed. The second part of the chapter introduces Field-Programmable Gate Arrays (FPGAs) and Application-Specific Integrated Circuits (ASICs). FPGAs are likened to flexible, customizable digital playgrounds, while ASICs are portrayed as purpose-built superheroes tailored for specific tasks. The discussion highlights the unique strengths of FPGAs in rapid prototyping and adaptability, while ASICs excel in energy efficiency and performance for specific applications. The chapter concludes by presenting a hybrid approach that combines FPGAs and ASICs in the development of real-time AI, leveraging flexibility and efficiency for optimal outcomes.

Real-time AI refers to the capability of artificial intelligence systems to process and respond to data instantaneously, with minimal latency or delay. In a real-time AI system, the processing and decision-making occur within a timeframe that is imperceptible to human users, typically on the order of milliseconds to microseconds. This rapid response time is crucial in applications where timely and instantaneous decisions are essential.

Real-time AI systems operate with low latency, meaning there is minimal delay between input data being received and the system generating a response. This low latency is essential in applications where quick decisions or actions are required.

Real-time AI systems make decisions or predictions almost instantaneously. This is particularly important in scenarios like autonomous vehicles, industrial automation, or medical diagnostics, where quick responses to changing conditions are critical.

Real-time AI involves continuous data processing, where the system analyzes and acts upon incoming data in real-time. This contrasts with batch processing, where data is collected over time and processed in discrete chunks.

Real-time AI systems are often designed to adapt dynamically to changing conditions. They can quickly adjust their responses based on new information, making them well-suited for applications in dynamic and unpredictable environments.

Real-time AI is commonly used in applications where time is of the essence, such as:

- **Autonomous Vehicles:** Quick decision-making is crucial for navigation and avoiding obstacles.
- **Financial Trading:** Rapid analysis of market data for timely trading decisions.
- **Healthcare Monitoring:** Immediate analysis of patient data for early detection of anomalies.
- **Industrial Automation:** Swift response to changes in manufacturing processes.
- **Sensor Integration:** Many real-time AI applications involve the integration of sensors that continuously provide data.

The AI system processes this incoming sensor data in real-time to make informed decisions.

- **Edge Computing:** Real-time AI often leverages edge computing, where processing occurs closer to the data source rather than relying on centralized cloud servers. Edge computing reduces latency and allows for faster responses in applications such as smart devices and IoT.
- **Efficient Algorithms:** Real-time AI algorithms are designed for efficiency and speed. These algorithms prioritize quick computations to ensure timely responses without sacrificing accuracy.

Real-time AI is employed in a wide range of applications, including:

- **Speech and Image Recognition:** For instant identification and response.
- **Fraud Detection:** Quick identification of potentially fraudulent transactions.
- **Video Surveillance:** Immediate analysis of video feeds for security purposes.
- **Gaming:** In-game decision-making and responsiveness.

Real-time AI focuses on achieving rapid, near-instantaneous decision-making, making it suitable for applications where timely responses are critical for effectiveness and safety.

Now imagine you have a piece of technology that can be customized for different tasks on the fly, almost like a magical shape-shifter. That's the essence of **Field-Programmable Gate Arrays**, or **FPGAs**.

Think of an FPGA as a playground filled with LEGO bricks, each representing a basic building block of digital circuits. Unlike fixed circuits in traditional electronics, FPGAs allow you to rearrange and configure these digital LEGO bricks to create different structures.

FPGAs are incredibly flexible. You can program them to perform specific tasks or computations based on your needs. It's like having a versatile tool that you can reconfigure for different jobs – today it's a calculator, tomorrow it's a graphics processor.

FPGAs are fantastic for rapid prototyping. Engineers and designers can use FPGAs to quickly test and iterate their ideas without the need to create custom chips for each experiment. It's like having a testing ground where you can tweak and refine your digital creations in real-time.

Suppose you're designing a new gadget – a smartwatch, for instance. FPGAs allow engineers to prototype the electronic components of the smartwatch and experiment with different functionalities before committing to a fixed design. It's like trying on different outfits before choosing the perfect one.

The reconfigurability of FPGAs is their magical quality. They can adapt to various applications, making them invaluable in scenarios where flexibility and customization are key.

Now, let's switch gears to **ASICs (Application-Specific Integrated Circuits)**, which are like the specialized superheroes of the tech world.

Application-Specific Integrated Circuits, or ASICs, are custom-made chips designed for a specific purpose. Imagine having a superhero with powers perfectly suited for a particular mission – ASICs are like that superhero, tailored for a specific task or application.

ASICs are incredibly efficient because they are purpose-built. Suppose you need a chip for a fitness tracker – an ASIC can be designed to precisely handle the computations needed for tracking steps, heart rate, and other fitness metrics. This specialization makes ASICs powerful and energy-efficient.

Since ASICs are created for a particular job, they can outperform general-purpose processors in that specific task. It's like having a chef's knife that excels at slicing and dicing, while a Swiss army knife, like a general-purpose processor, may handle many tasks adequately but not as efficiently.

ASICs integrate all the necessary components into a single chip. This integration enhances performance and reduces the need for external components. It's like having a superhero with all the essential tools and gadgets built into their suit.

ASICs are prevalent in many electronic devices, from smartphones to routers. Whenever you have a device that needs to perform a specific function exceptionally well, there's a good chance it relies on an ASIC.

FPGAs are like dynamic LEGO playgrounds, allowing for flexible and customizable digital configurations, while ASICs are purpose-built superheroes designed for specific tasks, offering unmatched efficiency and performance. Each has its unique strengths, and their roles complement each other in the ever-evolving landscape of technology.

Real-time AI requires quick and efficient processing of complex computations. Field-Programmable Gate Arrays (FPGAs) and Application-Specific Integrated Circuits (ASICs) play crucial roles in the development of real-time AI by offering specialized hardware solutions tailored to the demands of rapid and efficient processing.

FPGAs can be programmed to accelerate specific AI workloads, making them well-suited for real-time inference tasks. The flexibility of FPGAs allows developers to optimize and adapt the hardware architecture to the requirements of different AI models. ASICs, being custom-designed for specific AI tasks, excel in accelerated inference. Their optimized architecture allows for streamlined processing of neural network computations, leading to enhanced performance and reduced latency.

FPGAs can be configured to exploit parallelism, a key aspect of AI computations. This allows for the simultaneous execution of multiple operations, improving the overall processing speed and responsiveness of real-time AI applications. ASICs are inherently parallel processors, with custom-designed circuits optimized for the parallel nature of neural network computations. This parallelism significantly enhances the speed and efficiency of real-time AI tasks.

The reconfigurability of FPGAs allows developers to fine-tune the hardware architecture for minimal latency. FPGAs can be adapted to specific real-time requirements, making them suitable for applications where low latency is critical, such as autonomous vehicles and industrial automation. ASICs, being purpose-built for specific AI tasks, are optimized to minimize latency. Their integrated and specialized design enables them to process AI workloads with minimal delay, making them well-suited for real-time applications like image recognition or natural language processing.

FPGAs offer power efficiency through their flexibility. Developers can optimize the hardware configuration for specific tasks, ensuring that the FPGA consumes only the power necessary for the required computations. ASICs are known for their high power efficiency due to their tailored design. By eliminating unnecessary components and focusing solely on the required computations, ASICs provide a power-efficient solution for real-time AI applications, crucial for mobile devices and edge computing.

FPGAs provide a level of flexibility that allows developers to customize the hardware for specific AI models. This adaptability is valuable in scenarios where different real-time AI applications may have diverse computational requirements. ASICs, with their custom design, are specifically tailored to execute predefined neural network architectures efficiently. This level of customization enhances their performance in real-time AI applications that require dedicated hardware for specific models.

FPGAs are suitable for embedded systems and edge computing due to their flexibility and adaptability. They can be programmed to handle AI workloads directly on the edge, reducing the need for sending data to centralized servers. ASICs are well-suited for edge computing due to their power efficiency and optimized design.

They enable the deployment of real-time AI models directly on edge devices, reducing latency and bandwidth requirements.

A trend in real-time AI development involves hybrid approaches that combine the strengths of both FPGAs and ASICs. This may involve using FPGAs for prototyping and flexibility during development, followed by ASIC implementation for mass production, combining the benefits of flexibility and efficiency.

FPGAs and ASICs play complementary roles in the development of real-time AI, offering flexibility, customization, efficiency, and optimized performance. Their unique characteristics make them valuable components in the hardware ecosystem, contributing to the advancement of AI applications that demand real-time processing and responsiveness.

Chapter 17: Financial markets and trading

> Machine learning (ML) is changing virtually every aspect of our lives. Today ML algorithms accomplish tasks that until recently only expert humans could perform. As it relates to finance, this is the most exciting time to adopt a disruptive technology that will transform how everyone invests for generations.
>
> Marcos López de Prado, *Advances in Financial Machine Learning*

The chapter delves into the historical evolution of finance from an art to a science, tracing the shift from speculative rules outlined by Joseph de la Vega in the 17th century to the pioneering work of Louis Bachelier in introducing mathematical models for valuing stock options in the early 20th century. The narrative extends to the computerization of financial markets in the 1970s, with the introduction of electronic trading systems and the subsequent rise of algorithmic trading strategies. The chapter explores the challenges and transformative impact of the electronification of trading, highlighting incidents like the 2010 flash crash and the consequences of algorithmic anomalies. It also addresses the increasing adoption of artificial intelligence (AI) in hedge funds, emphasizing the role of AI in informing investment decisions, generating trading ideas, optimizing portfolios, and automating trade execution. The promising performance of AI hedge funds is noted, and the challenges of explaining AI-based approaches to investors are discussed, pointing to the ongoing transformation and reshaping of the finance industry through the convergence of technology and artificial intelligence.

At the time when Joseph de la Vega (ca. 1650-1692) was writing his masterpiece *Confusion de Confusiones* about the Amsterdam Stock Exchange, finance was an art rather than a science. He tried to make it more precise by formulating some rules:

> The first rule in speculation is: Never advise anyone to buy or sell shares. Where guessing correctly is a form of witchcraft, counsel cannot be put on airs.

> The second rule: Accept both your profits and regrets. It is best to seize what comes to hand when it comes, and not expect that your good fortune and the favourable circumstances will last.

> The third rule: Profit in the share market is goblin treasure: at one moment, it is carbuncles, the next it is coal; one moment diamonds, and the next pebbles. Sometimes, they are the tears that Aurora leaves on the sweet morning's grass, at other times, they are just tears.

> The fourth rule: He who wishes to become rich from this game must have both money and patience.

Amsterdam stock exchange.

Louis Bachelier (1870-1946) was not satisfied with such imprecise science. In his doctoral thesis he introduced the first mathematical model of Brownian motion and its use for valuing stock options. Advanced mathematics was used for the first time in the study of finance.

Bachelier was ahead of his time. *Mathematical finance* emerged as a discipline decades later, in the 1970s, following the Nobel prize-winning work of Fischer Black (1938-1995), Myron Scholes (b. 1941), and Robert Merton (b. 1944) on option pricing theory.

Computerization of the order flow in financial markets began at around the same time, in the early 1970s, when the New York Stock Exchange introduced the "designated order turnaround" system (DOT). The system allowed for the routing of orders electronically to the proper trading post. The financial landscape was changed again with the emergence of electronic communication networks (ECNs) in the 1990s, which allowed for trading of stock and currencies outside of traditional exchanges. This increased market liquidity led to institutional traders splitting up orders according to computer algorithms so they could execute orders at a better price.

As more electronic markets opened, new algorithmic trading strategies were introduced. These strategies are more easily implemented by computers, because machines can react more rapidly to temporary mispricing and examine prices from several markets simultaneously.

Robert Greifeld (b. 1957), the CEO of NASDAQ, proclaimed in April 2011:

> It is over. The trading that existed down the centuries has died. We have an electronic market today. It is the present. It is the future.

Electronification of trading was not without its problems.

On 6th May, 2010, the so-called *flash crash* took place. Stock indices, such as the S&P 500, Dow Jones Industrial Average, and Nasdaq Composite, collapsed and rebounded very rapidly. The Dow Jones Industrial Average had its second biggest intraday point decline (from the opening) up to that point, plunging 998.5 points (about 9%), most within minutes, only to recover a large part of the loss. It was also the second-largest intraday point swing (difference between intraday high and intraday low) up to that point, at 1,010.14 points. The prices of stocks, stock index futures, options, and exchange-traded funds (ETFs) were volatile, thus trading volume spiked. A CFTC 2014 report described it as one of the most turbulent periods in the history of financial markets.

The British trader Navinder Singh Sarao (b. 1978) was sentenced to a year of home imprisonment after he pleaded guilty to "spoofing" charges and subsequently co-operated with an ongoing US crackdown on abusive trading practices. Sarao had admitted in 2016 that he manipulated the market in E-Mini S&P 500 futures over five years ago by rapidly placing and withdrawing orders to push prices up and down, an illegal tactic called spoofing.

In August 2012, New York Times reported that

> Knight Trading Program Ran Amok, With No 'Off' Switch
>
> When computerized stock trading runs amok, as it did this week on Wall Street, the firm responsible typically can jump in and hit a kill switch.
>
> But as a torrent of faulty trades spewed Wednesday morning from a Knight Capital Group trading program, no one at the firm managed to stop it for more than a half-hour.
>
> ...
>
> On Friday, Knight, which in the last decade grew into a leading broker for American stocks, climbed off the mat, securing emergency financing that allowed it to continue operating for the day. It also enticed some of its customers to resume sending client stock trades, two days after it disclosed a possibly fatal $440 million loss from the software problem. But it faced a desperate weekend of manoeuvring to find a more permanent solution for its woes. Knight's

short-term financing was meant to keep it alive until Monday, when its executives and advisers hope to have deals completed to remove any doubt about the firm's future.

Still, electronification of capital markets continued. Electronic trading is now most advanced in those markets in which assets are most standardized and highly liquid – in particular cash equities, futures, CDS indices, and FX spot. In some markets, an increase in electronic trading has been driven directly by technological improvements that have facilitated a reduction in the marginal cost of providing intermediation services and lowered the barriers to entry for companies with a technology advantage. In others, still, it has been catalyzed by regulatory change.

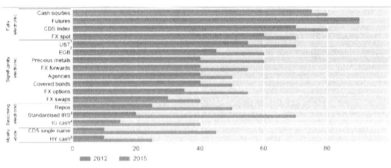

State of electronification in various asset classes. Source: *Electronic trading in fixed income markets* by Bank for International Settlements (January 2016).

Electronification itself is but a step on the way towards AI adoption.

In September 2018, BarclayHedge's Hedge Fund Sentiment Survey found that over half of hedge fund respondents (56%) used AI to inform investment decisions – nearly triple the 20% reported a year earlier. Around two-thirds of those using AI were doing so to generate trading ideas and optimize portfolios. Over a quarter were using it to automate trade execution, according to the survey.

The early results are promising. For example, the Eurekahedge AI Hedge Fund Index slightly outperformed the flagship Eurekahedge Hedge Fund Index in both 2017 and 2018. Moreover, the Eurekahedge Hedge Fund Index decreased by 4% in the fourth quarter of 2018, while the Eurekahedge AI Hedge Fund Index was flat for the period.

Peter Salvage of BNY Mellon wrote in March 2019:

> Hedge funds' use of AI is accelerating and reshaping the industry, particularly in investing cost models and recruitment. Managers also face challenges to explain new AI-based approaches to investors. Given the strategies are the byproduct of super computers crunching billions of data points and learning how to adjust to markets in real-time, explaining how returns are generated is pushing the boundaries of human comprehension.

Chapter 19: Shipping and logistics

> Ships are technically sophisticated, high value assets (larger hi-tech vessels can cost over US $200 million to build), and the operation of merchant ships generates an estimated annual income of over half a trillion US dollar in freight rates.
>
> International Chamber of Shipping

The chapter explores the transformative potential of artificial intelligence (AI) in the shipping industry, a sector that handles around 90% of global trade. AI applications in shipping are predicted to revolutionize operations, offering a strategic advantage to innovators in the field. Predictive maintenance (PdM), enabled by AI algorithms, emerges as a crucial strategy to proactively schedule corrective maintenance, minimizing downtime and associated costs for colossal vessels. Intelligent scheduling, simplified by recent AI advances, enhances vessel turnaround times and high-berth productivity, critical for competitive advantage in container terminals. Big Data and real-time analytics are expected to bring about "smart ships" capable of communication through nanotechnology and ultra-sensitive monitoring, transforming performance, productivity, and safety. The scope of AI extends beyond maintenance and scheduling to autonomous shipping, route optimization, weather forecasting, and fuel efficiency improvements, promising benefits in efficiency, environmental sustainability, and safety. However, ethical considerations such as job displacement and cybersecurity must be addressed to ensure responsible navigation into this AI-infused maritime future. In conclusion, the shipping industry is on the cusp of a new era where human ingenuity collaborates

with AI technologies for enhanced efficiency, safety, and sustainability.

According to the International Chamber of Shipping, the international shipping industry carries around 90% of world trade. "Ships are technically sophisticated, high value assets (larger hi-tech vessels can cost over US $200 million to build), and the operation of merchant ships generates an estimated annual income of over half a trillion US dollar in freight rates."[3]

A successful application of AI to shipping technology is predicted to revolutionize this critical mode of transportation and bring the innovator a strategic advantage over the rest of the industry.

According to Lloyd's Maritime Academy, AI "is becoming increasingly important for the maritime industry. The rise of automation in the maritime supply chain along with the demand for more autonomous shipping has led to an increase in the demand for AI."[4] Among the most promising applications of AI within shipping they highlight predictive maintenance, intelligence scheduling, and real-time analytics.

Predictive Maintenance (PdM) emerges as a crucial strategy in addressing maintenance challenges, aiming to minimize downtime and associated costs. The maritime sector, with its colossal vessels, encounters unique challenges in maintaining the health of onboard machinery. PdM, enabled by AI algorithms, allows for the proactive scheduling of corrective maintenance before ships embark on open waters. The AI-based system predicts potential failures in advance, empowering maritime workers to optimize maintenance cycles. This not only saves costs but also enhances productivity, reduces overhead expenses, and enables the strategic warehousing of spare parts.

---

[3] Quoted from http://www.ics-shipping.org/shipping-facts/shipping-and-world-trade

[4] Quoted from http://www.lloydsmaritimeacademy.com/event/artificial-intelligence-in-shipping-distance-learning-course

Intelligent scheduling enables faster turnaround time of vessels and high-berth productivity – "paramount factors in container terminals for assuming competitive advantage in the shipping industry. [...] Vessel scheduling/berthing system in a container terminal is regarded as a very complex dynamic application in today's business world."[5] Recent advances in AI can dramatically simplify this process leading to significant improvements in efficiency and cost reductions. Intelligent scheduling stands as a beacon for optimizing vessel turnaround times and high-berth productivity, critical factors for gaining a competitive edge in the shipping industry. The traditional complexities associated with vessel scheduling/berthing systems in container terminals are being tackled with recent advances in AI. The deployment of AI can streamline this intricate process, leading to substantial improvements in efficiency and cost reductions. This transformation is not merely about faster turnarounds but about redefining how vessels seamlessly navigate the complex dynamics of modern container terminals.

Big Data and **real-time analytics** are predicted to dramatically transform shipping. "A world where ships can 'talk.' It may sound like a tagline for a science fiction movie but it's not as far-fetched as it sounds – such ships could be coming to a sea near you within 10 years. [...] These 'smart ships' of the not-so-distant future will be able to 'talk' through the use of nanotechnology in paints, coatings, and materials, while ultra-sensitive monitoring through the use of acoustic fibres will allow the detection of minute changes in vibrations. In this brave new maritime world voyage data and data from ship strictures, components, and machinery will be collated and used to enhance performance, productivity, and crucially, safety," according to an expert risk article by Allianz.[6]

---

[5] Prasanna Lokuge, Damminda Alahakoon. *Improving the adaptability in automated vessel scheduling in container ports using intelligent software agents.* European Journal of Operational Research, 177(3):1985-2015.
[6] Quoted from https://www.agcs.allianz.com/insights/expert-risk-articles/how-big-data-will-transform-shipping/

Looking ahead, the scope of AI in shipping extends far beyond predictive maintenance, intelligent scheduling, and real-time analytics. From autonomous shipping and route optimization to weather forecasting and fuel efficiency improvements, AI applications are poised to touch every aspect of maritime operations. Moreover, the potential benefits ripple beyond efficiency gains to include environmental sustainability and enhanced safety protocols.

As we sail into this AI-infused maritime future, it is imperative to navigate responsibly. Considerations of ethics in AI, such as potential job displacement and the need for robust cybersecurity measures, must be addressed. Striking a balance between technological advancement and ethical considerations ensures that the industry benefits not only economically but also ethically.

In conclusion, the winds of change are propelling the shipping industry into uncharted territories, guided by the transformative potential of AI. Predictive maintenance, intelligent scheduling, and real-time analytics are the vanguards of this revolution, but the horizon promises even more innovations. The collaboration of human ingenuity with AI technologies will define a new era of shipping, where efficiency, safety, and sustainability harmoniously navigate the seas of tomorrow.

Chapter 20: Life sciences

The productivity of the pharmaceutical industry is on the decline. Failure rates in clinical trials exceed 90% after therapies are tested in model organisms, and the cost to develop a new drug exceeds $2.6 billion. Recent advances in artificial intelligence (AI) may help reverse this trend and accelerate and improve pharmaceutical R&D.

Alex Zhavoronkov, *Artificial Intelligence for Drug Discovery, Biomarker Development, and Generation of Novel Chemistry*

The chapter explores the challenges in drug discovery highlighted by Eroom's Law, which posits that the process becomes slower and more difficult over time, leading to doubling costs every nine years. It identifies causes such as the "better than the Beatles" problem, cautious regulators, the inclination to throw more resources at the problem, and an overestimation of basic research and brute force methods. The advent of artificial intelligence (AI), particularly machine learning (ML) and deep learning (DL), offers a transformative solution to the sluggish drug discovery process. ML and DL enable virtual screening of big data to predict therapeutic targets and identify drug candidates, reducing costs and time. The chapter delves into the significance of proteins, the building blocks of life, and their 3D structure's role in drug discovery. It discusses the historical challenge of predicting protein structures, with a breakthrough achieved by DeepMind's AlphaFold in the CASP13 experiment. The AI system demonstrated remarkable precision in predicting protein structures, paving the way for accelerated drug discovery by replacing slow and expensive experimental methods with faster computer simulations. The chapter underscores the potential of AI to revolutionize drug discovery, offering speed, precision, and cost-effectiveness.

We have already encountered Moore's law in the chapter on computers. In drug discovery, a different law is observed – Eroom's law – which is Moore's law spelled backwards. It refers, as you'd fear, to processes that are getting slower and more difficult over time. The following graph illustrates Eroom's law:

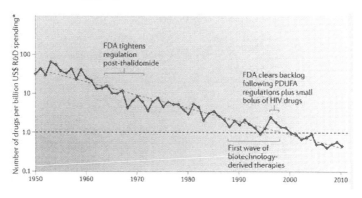

Image source: Wikipedia.

Drug discovery is becoming slower and more expensive over time, despite improvements in technology (such as high-throughput screening, biotechnology, combinatorial chemistry, and computational drug design). The cost of developing a new drug roughly doubles every nine years (inflation-adjusted).

The article proposing and naming the law attributes it to four main causes:

- *The 'better than the Beatles' problem.* Imagine how hard it would be to achieve commercial success with new pop songs if any new song had to be better than the Beatles, if the entire Beatles catalogue was available for free, and if people did not get bored with old Beatles records. Something similar applies to the discovery and development of new drugs. Yesterday's blockbuster is today's generic. An ever-

160

improving back catalogue of approved medicines increases the complexity of the development process for new drugs, and raises the evidential hurdles for approval, adoption and reimbursement.

- *The 'cautious regulator' problem.* Progressive lowering of the risk tolerance of drug regulatory agencies obviously raises the bar for the introduction of new drugs, and could substantially increase the associated costs of R&D.

- *The 'throw money at it' tendency* – the tendency to add human resources and other resources to R&D, which – until recent years – has generally led to a rise in R&D spending in major companies, and for the industry overall.

- *The 'basic research – brute force' bias* – the tendency to overestimate the ability of advances in basic research (particularly in molecular biology) and brute force screening methods (embodied in the first few steps of the standard discovery and preclinical research process) to increase the probability that a molecule will be safe and effective in clinical trials.

Novel identification of compounds and targets is a laborious and uncertain process which requires in-depth understanding of cellular and molecular pathology. The development stage involves screening of compounds and molecules with the potential to act favourably on a desired therapeutic target whilst exerting minimal effect on others. The most promising compounds are progressed to the next stage of the study.

In contrast to the conventional approach, AI, particularly ML, uses virtual screening of big data to predict therapeutic targets and identify suitable drug candidates for the disease variant. ML is capable of analyzing vast amounts of information from areas such as gene mapping, pharmacokinetics, solubility profiles and receptor affinities to predict properties of novel agents with their target counterparts. Meanwhile, DL is evolving in the discovery of de novo compounds by proposing new synthesis routes of previously discovered molecules and creating molecules not previously synthesized ever before. Similarly, the risk-based algorithms of ML/DL can also be used to screen agents and predict therapeutic efficacy and toxicity. Overall, computer-based learning with AI enabled pharmaceutical companies to reduce huge expense, resources utilized and time taken for product synthesis from the beginning of the drug pipeline.

Proteins are the building blocks of life. They are large, complex molecules comprised of one or more long chains of *amino acids*. There are 20 different types of amino acids that can be combined to make a protein. Amino acids are coded by combinations of three DNA building blocks (*nucleotides*), determined by the sequence of genes.

Every cell in the human body contains proteins. Proteins are the chief actors within the cell: they carry out the duties specified by the information contained in the genetic code.

Proteins play many critical roles in the body:

Function	Description	Example
Antibody	Antibodies are used by the immune system to identify and neutralize foreign objects such as pathogenic bacteria and viruses.	Immunoglobulin G (IgG)
Enzyme	Enzymes accelerate chemical reactions. They also assist with the formation of new molecules by reading the genetic information stored in DNA.	Glucosidase
Messenger	Messenger proteins, such as some types of hormones, transmit signals to coordinate biological processes between different cells, tissues, and organs.	Growth hormone
Structural component	These proteins provide structure and support for cells. On a larger scale, they also allow the body to move.	Actin
Transport / storage	These proteins bind and carry atoms and small molecules within cells and throughout the body.	Ferritin

A major milestone in protein science was the thermodynamic hypothesis of Christian Anfinsen (1916-1995) and his colleagues. From his experiments on ribonuclease, Anfinsen concluded that the native structure of a protein is the thermodynamically stable structure; it depends only on the amino acid sequence and on the conditions of solution, and not on the kinetic folding route. In particular, the native structure does not depend on whether the protein was synthesized biologically on a ribosome or with the help of chaperone molecules, or if, instead, the protein was simply refolded as an isolated molecule in a test tube.

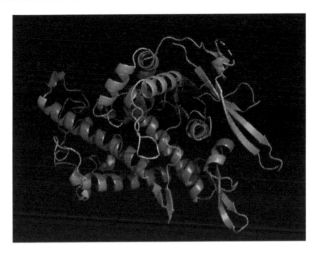

A protein's function is determined by its 3D shape. Image source: DeepMind.

What a protein does largely depends on its structure. A major goal of computational biology has been to predict a protein's 3D structure from its amino acid sequence – the *protein folding problem.* A solution to this problem could help accelerate drug discovery by replacing slow, expensive structural biology experiments with faster, cheaper computer simulations. It would also enable researchers to deduce protein function from genome sequences. The protein folding problem stood as a grand challenge in biology for the past 50 years.

Starting in 1994, the performance of current approaches to the protein folding problem is assessed biannually in the CASP experiment (Critical Assessment of Techniques for Protein Structure Prediction).

In December 2018, CASP13 made headlines when it was won by AlphaFold, an artificial intelligence program created by DeepMind. AlphaFold was designed as a deep learning system:

> Central to AlphaFold is a distance map predictor implemented as a very deep residual neural network with 220 residual blocks processing a representation of dimensionality 64 x 64 x 128 – corresponding to input features calculated from two 64 amino acid fragments. Each residual block has three layers including a 3 x 3 dilated convolutional layer – the blocks cycle through dilation of values 1, 2, 4, and 8. In total the model has 21 million parameters. The network uses a combination of 1D and 2D inputs, including evolutionary profiles from different sources and co-evolution features. Alongside a distance map in the form of a very finely-grained histogram of distances, AlphaFold predicts Φ and Ψ angles for each residue which are used to create the initial predicted 3D structure. The AlphaFold authors concluded that the depth of the model, its large crop size, the large training set of roughly 29,000 proteins, modern Deep Learning techniques, and the richness of information from the predicted histogram of distances helped AlphaFold achieve a high contact map prediction precision.

In November 2020, an improved version of AlphaFold won CASP14. A key part of the 2020 system are two modules, based on a transformer design, which are used to progressively refine a vector of information for each relationship between an amino acid residue of the protein and another amino acid residue (these relationships are represented by the array shown in green); and between each amino acid position and each different sequence in the input sequence alignment (these relationships are represented by the array shown in red). As the iteration progresses, according to one report, the "attention algorithm ... mimics the way a person might assemble a jugsaw puzzle: first connecting pieces in small clumps – in this case clusters of amino acids – and then searching for ways to join the clumps in a larger whole".

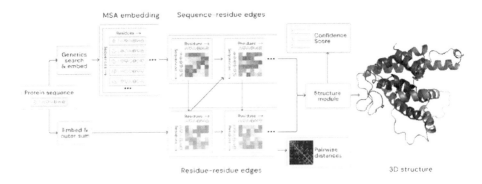

Image source: DeepMind.

Professor John Moult, co-founder and chair of CASP, University of Maryland, expressed his feelings about this breakthrough:

> We have been stuck on this one problem – how do proteins fold up – for nearly 50 years. To see DeepMind produce a solution for this, having worked personally on this problem for so long and after so many stops and starts, wondering if we'd ever get there, is a very special moment.

According to Arthur D. Levinson, Founder and CEO of Calico,

> AlphaFold is a once in a generation advance, predicting protein structures with incredible speed and precision. This leap forward demonstrates how computational methods are poised to transform research in biology and hold much promise for accelerating the drug discovery process.

Conclusion

Left to right: Yann LeCun, Yoshua Bengio, Geoffrey Hinton. Image source: the Association for Computing Machinery (ACM).

There is no Nobel Prize in computing. The ACM A. M. Turing Award given by the Association for Computing Machinery (ACM) for contributions "of a lasting and major technical importance to the computer field" is as close to a Nobel Prize as it gets. The award is named after Alan Turing. It carries a $1 million prize, with financial support provided by Google.

ACM presented the 2018 A.M. Turing Award at its annual Awards Banquet on 15th June in San Francisco. There were three recipients: Yoshua Bengio, Geoffrey Hinton, and Yann LeCun.

The ACM President Cherri M. Pancake explained ACM's choice:

> Artificial intelligence is now one of the fastest-growing areas in all of science and one of the most talked-about topics in society. The growth of and interest in AI is due, in no small part, to the recent advances in deep learning for which

Bengio, Hinton and LeCun laid the foundation. These technologies are used by billions of people. Anyone who has a smartphone in their pocket can tangibly experience advances in natural language processing and computer vision that were not possible just 10 years ago. In addition to the products we use every day, new advances in deep learning have given scientists powerful new tools – in areas ranging from medicine, to astronomy, to materials science.

On 27th November, 2019, a curious article was published on BBC News:

> A master player of the Chinese strategy game Go has decided to retire, due to the rise of artificial intelligence that "cannot be defeated."

This article was about Lee Sedol, whom we have met at the beginning of this book. He remained the only human to ever beat the AlphaGo software.

> The South Korean said he had decided to retire after realising: "I'm not at the top even if I become the number one."

In May 2023, Hinton announced his resignation from Google to be able to "freely speak out about the risks of AI." On 8 October, 2023, when speaking to CBS News' Scott Pelley, Hinton stated: "I think we're moving into a period when for the first time ever we may have things more intelligent than us."

> Scott Pelley: You believe they can understand?
>
> Geoffrey Hinton: Yes.
>
> SP: You believe they are intelligent?
>
> GH: Yes.
>
> SP: You believe these systems have experiences of their own and can make decisions based on those experiences?

GH: In the same sense as people do, yes.

SP: Are they conscious?

GH: I think they probably don't have much self-awareness at present. So, in that sense, I don't think they're conscious.

SP: Will they have self-awareness, consciousness?

GH: Oh, yes.

SP: Yes?

GH: Oh, yes. I think they will, in time.

SP: And so human beings will be the second most intelligent beings on the planet?

GH: Yeah.

In June 2023, Insilico Medicine's novel AI-generated small molecule inhibitor drug represented a new milestone in pharmaceutical drug development. The world's first AI-generated anti-fibrotic small molecule inhibitor medicine has been administered to the first human patients. Phase II clinical trials in the US and China are now underway for INS018_055, Insilico Medicine's potentially first-in-class oral drug candidate. It is hoped that this drug will help people with the rare lung disease, idiopathic pulmonary fibrosis (IPF). More AI-generated drugs for rare and common diseases are now on their way.

The Machine Learning Institute (MLI)

Hi, my name is Neil Clive Fowler, I'm Founder and Managing Director of World Business Strategies (WBS) Training. Our company organizes workshops and conferences for major financial institutions.

Jointly with our partners, Thalesians Ltd and Thalesians Marine Ltd, we founded the Machine Learning Institute (MLI) on 3 December 2018, with the launch of our first cohort of students. In 2023, we have just welcomed our 10th cohort!

MLI is the world's most comprehensive professional training in machine learning and artificial intelligence with a particular focus on finance and trading. We realize that not everyone can dedicate a full year of their life to study ML/AI at university at MSc level or three years at PhD level. Therefore, we have created this seven-month part-time course, which you can do twice a week in the evenings, without leaving your job.

We cover the foundations of ML/AI, as well as the most exciting recently developed topics, such as:

- Training LLMs for quant finance,

- Generative modelling with normalizing flows: foundations and applications,
- Foundation NLP models for ESG data extraction,
- Building neural networks,
- Deep learning, machine learning, and consciousness.

We will also support you with our industry-leading lifelong learning on the completion of the course.

At the end of the course students are awarded the prestigious MLI certificate. All lectures are recorded and can be accessed at any time in your personalized educational portal. You can qualify from anywhere in the world, on a part-time basis, with fully flexible study options.

Over 500 alumni have now chosen the MLI, in over 40 countries, to become industry-leading ML and AI expert. We are looking forward to welcoming you as our student in continuation of your ML/AI journey.

For more information and to apply for the MLI certification programme, we invite you to visit

https://mlinstitute.org/